PLAXTON
A Century of Innovation

STEWART J. BROWN

Ian Allan PUBLISHING

Contents

Previous page: One of Plaxton's biggest customers in the 1950s was Wallace Arnold. This AEC Reliance, one of a batch of 17 delivered in 1958, has survived in preservation. It is a 41-seater. *Plaxton*

Right: This immaculate Leyland Tiger PS1 has been owned since new by the same company — John Smith & Sons of Thirsk. Out of use for many years, it has been painstakingly restored to its original condition. *Plaxton*

First published 2007

ISBN (10) 0 7110 3209 2

ISBN (13) 978 0 7110 3209 5

Published by Ian Allan Publishing

an imprint of Ian Allan Publishing Ltd, Hersham, Surrey KT12 4RG

Printed in England by Ian Allan Printing Ltd, Hersham, Surrey KT12 4RG

Code: 0705/B

Visit the Ian Allan Publishing website at www.ianallanpublishing.com

Foreword

Plaxton has seen some remarkable and dramatic changes in recent years. That it has not only survived but is also prospering is a tribute to the enthusiasm, the skills and the commitment to succeed which have been demonstrated by everyone involved in creating the company we see today.

Few companies survive to celebrate 100 years in business. Today's stainless steel-framed coaches are a world away from the primitive wooden-framed charabancs built by F. W. Plaxton in the early years of the last century. They feature comforts which were unimaginable all those years ago — reclining seats, on-board entertainment systems, air-conditioning, even heating, which became commonplace only in the 1950s.

Over the last 100 years Plaxton has grown from being a small regional coachbuilder to a major supplier of coaches and buses to operators throughout the British Isles. It has achieved this through innovation — the original Panorama, for example, was a turning-point in coach design — and by being responsive to the needs of its customers.

But whatever the advances in design, in materials and in production methods there is continuity in the company's story, with production still being carried on in Scarborough, and still with a focus on the needs of a diverse range of generally small coach and bus businesses. The company's flexibility in production and its ability to deal with small family-run businesses as well as large nationwide transport groups have helped contribute to its success.

There can be few coach operators in Britain — my own business included — that have not operated a Plaxton at some time in their history, and in the pages that follow the story unfolds of one of the great successes in British coach and bus manufacturing.

Like a great many other bus and coach operators throughout the British Isles I am delighted that Plaxton is celebrating its centenary, and at the same time as acknowledging its past I wish the company and the people who have made it what it is a prosperous future.

Stephen R. Telling
Chairman and Chief Executive
Tellings Golden Miller Group

Acknowledgements

A great many people helped in the preparation of this book and in checking the text. Particular thanks are due to former Plaxton employees Charles Marshall, Stuart Pringle and Bob Walmsley, who generously shared their considerable knowledge of the company over very many years, and to Stephen Barber, formerly of Wallace Arnold. Any errors are mine, not theirs. *SJB*

Below: Weardale Motor Services operates this Leyland Leopard with Supreme body — still with its original paint finish more than 25 years after it left Plaxton's factory. *Plaxton*

ONE

From Cars to Coaches

THE Plaxton business has changed beyond all recognition over its 100-year history. For much of that time it has been one of Scarborough's major employers, and today it is the biggest private-sector employer in the town, with a workforce of over 300.

At times it has ranked among Europe's biggest coachbuilders, producing over 1,000 vehicles a year at its peak. But as the travel market has changed, so too has Plaxton's business. Production volumes are now more modest — around 650 in 2007 — and the focus is once again on quality rather than quantity.

In its early days Plaxton built bodies for motor cars — then affordable only by the rich. Today it builds a range of high-quality touring coaches and a new generation of low-floor buses.

The company's coaches — Panther, Paragon, Profile and Cheetah — make Plaxton the leader in the UK coach market, despite ever-increasing competition from manufacturers in Europe and further afield.

Two of its bus models — Centro and Primo — took to the roads only in 2006, the year in which the company opened a dedicated bus production facility alongside its modern coach production plant. These are both fully accessible low-floor models, and they build on the company's considerable expertise gained in the 1990s in producing the Pointer — one of the most successful body designs in the history of the British bus industry. Its other bus models are the Beaver and the Pronto — small vehicles used primarily for rural services or for community transport links. The Beaver has the distinction of being one of the longest-lived bus designs ever, having been launched in 1986.

Yet the Plaxton story starts not with coaches but with buildings. When Frederick William Plaxton set up in business in Bar Street, Scarborough, in 1907, it was as a joiner. Very quickly the business expanded, becoming a building contractor and taking on some major projects in the town, including the Futurist Cinema on the seafront, the Cumberland Hotel

and the Scarborough Girls' High School. The company also built Scarborough's famous Valley Bridge.

In these early years Frederick Plaxton was the driving force of the business and was a noted figure around Scarborough, often seen astride his horse as he travelled the town overseeing many of the building projects in which the company was involved.

Plaxton started building car bodies shortly before the outbreak of World War 1. During the conflict the company diversified into another area of the transport business, producing wooden parts for aircraft frames. By this time it had opened additional premises in the town, with an office on North Street, a timber store at James Place and a builder's yard in Alma Parade.

When the war ended there was an explosion of interest in motor vehicles — automotive technology had advanced rapidly in the war years, and many of those who served in the armed forces had acquired the skills necessary to work with cars, lorries and charabancs. Frederick Plaxton clearly saw a business opportunity, and in a new workshop designed for the purpose — Castle Works — began building bodies to meet the growing demand for cars and charabancs. At this stage bodywork was timber-framed, so it was a logical diversification by the company, using the expertise of a skilled workforce.

In the early 1920s Plaxton was producing as many as five car bodies a week on a range of chassis, many by makers long forgotten. These included Crossley, Daimler, Ford, Hillman, Lagonda, Rolls-Royce, Sunbeam and Willys-Knight. Plaxton was building high-quality bodies, and its work on Crossley chassis included cars for use by royalty. Plaxton-bodied Crossleys were used by the Prince of Wales and his entourage for a 1922 tour of Australia, and by the Duke of York for a visit to South Africa the following year, and then again for a New Zealand tour in 1926. King George V had a Crossley with a Plaxton limousine body in the mid-1920s, which was quite an endorsement for a small Yorkshire business — and an indication of the quality of the company's products. During the 1920s Plaxton had a car showroom in Leeds.

Alongside the cars Plaxton was building small numbers of charabancs for local operators, its first reputedly being on a Model T Ford chassis in 1920. Others were built on Italian Lancia chassis. A local Scarborough operator, Robinsons, bought Plaxton-bodied Lancias for its own fleet and for resale to other companies — an early large order from Robinson was for 23 bodies on Lancia chassis in the early 1920s.

The production of car bodywork continued into the 1930s, but coach-building became a greater part of the business. The 1929 depression

was a significant factor, but there were changes coming in the way cars were built, foreshadowed by the Ford Model T, which was produced on an assembly line. Mass-production was coming, and with it there would be no place for small specialist body-builders. Although car production had virtually ended by the early 1930s a number were produced during this period, predominantly on more expensive chassis such as Bentley and Daimler. Plaxton's final involvement with cars was the production of a seven-seat touring car built on light-van chassis in the late 1930s. Few were built.

But the company was still involved in larger vehicles. In the late 1920s there was a rapid move away from charabancs to coaches. On a charabanc each row of seats occupied the full width of the body, passengers entering by individual doors for each row. Charabancs were open to the weather, with a canvas top which could be pulled over the seating area to provide protection from the rain.

Coaches marked a significant advance, with two pairs of seats divided by a central gangway running the length of the vehicle, and usually just one entrance at the front or the rear, although some early coaches had two. The new generation of coaches also had fully enclosed bodywork, allowing comfortable touring in all weathers.

Plaxton was building both touring coaches and service buses from the early 1930s, albeit in small

Above: Plaxton's strength was the production of high-quality coaches. In its centenary year the mainstream models are the Panther, Paragon and Profile. This Panther, on a Volvo B12M chassis, is operated by Elcock Reisen of Telford, a long-standing user of Plaxton products. *Plaxton*

Above: In the 1920s Plaxton was primarily a builder of bodywork on cars and worked closely with Crossley, based in Manchester. This view shows two Crossleys on the Plaxton stand at the Motor Show in London's Olympia in the mid-1920s. Plaxton counted royalty among its customers for bodywork on Crossley chassis.
Plaxton

Right: Car production in the 1920s was a relatively small-scale business. Here workers put the finishing touches to a variety of cars ready for delivery to customers or to a distributor's showroom. *Plaxton*

Left: One of Plaxton's earliest charabanc bodies, built soon after the end of World War 1, was this example on the ubiquitous Model T Ford. The operator is unknown, but the charabanc carries a registration issued by the North Riding of Yorkshire, so it's fair to assume that the owner was fairly local, as was the case with the buyers of most early Plaxton products. *Plaxton*

Right: This stylish body was produced in the 1920s on a Renault chassis using the Weymann system, whereby the body was fabric-covered. Despite its size this was an estate car rather than a bus, with three doors on the offside and two on the nearside. It was produced by a short-lived business called F.W. Plaxton, Smith & Bianchi, formed to build Weymann-style bodywork. *Plaxton*

Left: A visit to New Zealand in 1927 by the Duke and Duchess of York — later to be King George V and Queen Elizabeth — involved the use of Crossley 18/50 models with Plaxton bodywork. *Plaxton*

Right and below: In 1935/6 Plaxton secured the contract from local operator United Automobile Services to supply 10 bodies for buses used on a seafront service in Scarborough. Fitted to 1928 ADC chassis, the bodies had centre entrances and full-width fronts, which created an image of modernity. The buses were stored during the war, but in 1949 the bodies were removed from the elderly ADC chassis and fitted to 1938 Leyland Tiger chassis, following which they operated on the seafront service until 1956. The Tiger bears a United (rather than Leyland) badge on the radiator. *Roy Marshall*

numbers and for locally based operators. In 1931 a Plaxton body won second prize in the section for single-deck buses in the commercial bodywork competition being held at that year's Motor Show in London's Olympia exhibition halls.

An early fleet order, at a time when most Plaxton customers were buying just one or two vehicles, came from United Automobile Services, one of the biggest operators of local bus services in North East England. United ran summer seafront services in Scarborough and turned to Plaxton in 1935 for the supply of 10 stylish full-fronted bodies for the buses used on this operation. These bodies were fitted to existing chassis — 1928 ADCs — but were of such sound construction that when the ADC chassis reached the end of their lives in 1949 the bodies were

transferred to 1938 Leyland Tiger chassis, continuing in use on the seafront service until 1956.

Coach travel was a growing business in the 1930s, and Plaxton was expanding. It was outgrowing its Castle Works and in 1936 built a new factory in Seamer Road, which opened in January 1937. This was a time when Plaxton coaches started to be seen further afield — not just in Yorkshire and the North East of England. The company started looking for business across the Pennines, appointing Lancashire Motor Traders of Manchester as a dealer. At the same time it established a dealership in London, appointing the Arlington Motor Co to handle its sales. Both companies would be Plaxton dealers for 50 years.

The company also changed its name, adding '& Son' to the established F. W. Plaxton title, as

Left: F. W. Plaxton junior (1920-95) — universally known as Eric — was the last member of the family to be involved in the business which bore his name. Involved in the running of the business from 1937 until he retired in 1988, he was a significant benefactor to Scarborough and in his will left funding for a new lifeboat for the town. In the company's centenary year work is in progress by the Joseph Rowntree Housing Trust on a development in the town to be called Plaxton Court, in recognition of significant funding provided by Eric's charitable trust. This is a 1981 photograph. *Plaxton*

Frederick William Plaxton junior — universally known as Eric — joined the business. On his father's death in 1957 Eric Plaxton assumed the position of Chairman and would be involved in running the company that carried his name for a further 31 years, retiring in 1988. F. W. Plaxton's daughter, Gladys, was also involved in the company.

As well as building bodies on new chassis in the late 1930s, Plaxton was also fitting bodies to older, reconditioned chassis.

The establishment of the Seamer Road works saw Plaxton start to adopt a range of standardised designs. The company's mid-1930s models often featured a stepped waist-rail and sloping window pillars, but in the late 1930s new designs appeared with a gently curved waist. Most coaches of this era had a sliding section in the roof that could be opened in good weather. On some Plaxton bodies a novel styling feature was the use of alternate-sized side pillars. The standard-width pillars, needed for structural strength, alternated with

Left: Gentle curves characterised most late-1930s coach bodies, and those built by Plaxton were no exception. This photograph shows a design known as the M2. It has drop-down windows with glazed louvers, to reduce draughts, and a sliding sunroof. The operator can be identified only as W&M. The winged device which surrounds the operator's initials was used by many Plaxton customers at this time. *Plaxton*

Right: Designs at Plaxton developed quickly in the late 1930s. This style, known as the D3, appeared towards the end of 1937. Note how the combination of thick and thin pillars creates the illusion of a huge main side window. Where the M2 had pronounced outward curvature on the lower rear panels, the D3 did not, and in this it anticipated postwar styling trends. This example is a 32-seater on a Leyland Tiger chassis. *Plaxton*

Below: The company's 1937 catalogue featured this rakish coach on the cover. A stylised representation of contemporary designs, it emphasised how the main side windows were grouped in pairs using thin intermediate pillars to create the effect of bigger windows — 20 years before the concept was turned into reality with the Panorama. *Plaxton*

thin stainless-steel pillars that created the visual effect of double-length panoramic windows — anticipating an even bolder move by Plaxton's designers 20 years later.

Another innovative styling feature on the typical half-cab coach body of the time was adding a fairing over the front nearside wheel, which created a streamlined effect and had the practical purpose of concealing the header tank for the Autovac fuel supply, which was a common fitting on coaches. The fairing impeded access to the engine and was hinged so that it could be swung clear of the bonnet.

Plaxton also tried streamlining the bodywork that it fitted to small normal-control chassis, by fitting a sloping front which swept up from the front wings. This, too, was a feature in which style outweighed practicality, and it made access to the

Above: A 1938 Leyland Tiger in the fleet of Bere Regis & District shows how Plaxton used a valance ahead of the entrance to improve the appearance of what was an untidy area on half-cab coaches. The valance concealed part of the bonnet from the view of boarding passengers. Various styles were used, some extending much further forward and being hinged so they could be swung clear of the bonnet when access to the engine was needed. This body has a fixed valance. Observe also the starting handle and the tiny nearside rear-view mirror. *Roy Marshall*

Left: A more austere style of body was fitted to this Tiger in the fleet of North East of England operator Heather Bell Services. It has a straight waist with just a slight curve below the rearmost window, while the front canopy extends roughly half the length of the driver's cab; as a result the nearside mirror has to be located further back than on bodies with full-length canopies. This view was recorded in Bishop Auckland in 1954, near the end of the Tiger's working life. *Roy Marshall*

Wood's Radio Luxury Coaches.

26, 30 & 32 SEATERS

TEL. NO.
BRIGHOUSE 1

TEL. NO.
LOW MOOR 95

Tariffs & Particulars on Application.

CHARLES WOOD L^{TD.} | 52, BRIGGATE — BRIGHOUSE
& TOWNGATE —— WYKE

Above: Some coach operators produced postcards to promote their business, among them Wood's of Brighouse, whose phone number was Brighouse 1. The coach is a Plaxton-bodied Dodge, a normal-control chassis on which the protruding bonnet has been disguised by locating the windscreen slightly further forward than normal and extending the front of the body down to meet the wings. Similar bodies were built on Bedford WTB chassis.
This coach was new in 1939.
Stephen Barber collection

engine bay awkward, even allowing for the fact that the streamlined panels were designed to be easily removed.

A notable variant of this style came in the postwar era when Plaxton converted the popular Bedford OB to a semi forward-control layout. This involved moving the driving position forward alongside the engine, pulling the steering column up to a more upright angle, and fitting a streamlined, full-fronted body, from which the OB's distinctive radiator protruded. This was a unique style and had the added benefit of making room for an extra seat alongside the engine opposite the driver.

Features such as these showed an appreciation of the importance of style in coach travel, something that has been a hallmark of Plaxton products down the years.

Typical coaches of the 1930s seated 26 on small chassis, such as the Bedford WTB or Dodge, or 32 on what were then considered full-size chassis, the 27ft-long Leyland Tiger or AEC Regal. Heaters were not a standard fitting and were fairly primitive when they were fitted, so coach passengers were often given travelling rugs for warmth on colder days.

In 1939 war broke out, and as a result coach

production in Britain came to an end, not just at Plaxton but at all other coachbuilders too. Some, Plaxton's big rival Duple included, were requisitioned to produce utility buses for essential war use, but Plaxton's modern Seamer Road factory was turned over to the production of munitions, controlled by the Ministry of Aircraft Production, for the duration of the conflict. Instead of manufacturing bodywork, Plaxton's production was utilised for more mundane but nonetheless essential items such as munitions boxes and other timber-framed structures for the military. A major factor in this was the exodus of a large proportion of the company's skilled labour force, both to the armed forces and to more specialist manufacturing such as aircraft production. During the war a large proportion of Plaxton's labour was provided by women, drafted in from the local area and from further afield.

Prior to the outbreak of war Plaxton had been working on a coach design with windscreens which would have incorporated curved glass, but that was shelved. Another project abandoned because of the war was a double-deck bus body — a strange diversification for a company which was building very few single-deck buses.

Left: The body on this 1939 Bedford OB anticipates Plaxton's postwar style, with a gently curved waist and slender window pillars. Indeed, only the mouldings identify this as a prewar body; note how similar they are to those on the Heather Bell Tiger and the Wood's Dodge, down to the short section which curves up from the main side flash to join the rear mouldings. This neat little coach was operated by Hargreaves of Hebden, near Skipton, and is seen in service in Grassington. *Roy Marshall*

Below: Plaxton's Seamer Road works was opened in 1937, as production outgrew the Castle Works site. The purpose-designed factory not only increased output but also improved efficiency. Seamer Road, in the foreground, nowadays forms part of the main A64 into Scarborough. Behind the factory is the LNER line from Scarborough to York. The site is now occupied by a trading estate. *Plaxton*

Expansion in the Postwar Boom

As soon as the war ended Plaxton immediately turned its attention to coaches once again, deliveries starting in early 1946. The company's first postwar bodies were elegant and were built on a wide range of chassis — AEC, Albion, Austin, Bedford, Commer, Crossley, Daimler, Dennis, Foden, Guy, Leyland, Maudslay and Seddon — at a time when only British-built chassis were available and no-one foresaw the dramatic changes to come in vehicle manufacturing.

Small coaches — Austins, Bedfords and Commers — typically seated 29. Bigger coaches seated 33. Specifications were simple by the standards of later days. A manually operated sliding door was standard — and could require some muscle power to pull it open. Ventilation was straightforward — the side windows could be opened a few inches by winding them down using a handle. The opening sunroof was still available as an option, although it would fall from favour at the start of the 1950s. A few coaches were fitted with radios, and a growing number had heaters — typically a large cylindrical radiator in a chromium-plated housing on the front bulkhead, produced by Clayton.

Bodywork was still timber-framed, with steel gussets. The chassis specification was simple too. A big six-cylinder engine, 7.4 litres and 100bhp in the Leyland Tiger, for example, was linked to a four-speed manual gearbox. Leaf suspension and vacuum brakes were standard. And the whole ensemble was relatively light, typically weighing between 6½ and 7 tons.

The 1940s saw Plaxton supplying a growing number of operators around the country, and securing business from some big-name companies. These included Wallace Arnold of Leeds, Hall Bros of South Shields, Robinsons of Great Harwood, Bullock of Cheadle, Northern Roadways of Glasgow, Ledgard of Leeds, Cotter of

Left: On postwar Bedford OBs Plaxton again offered a modified front end that concealed the model's normal-control layout. However, the driving position was also modified, locating the driver further forward and creating more room for passengers. The result was a stylish 29/30-seater, as demonstrated by this example in the fleet of Galley's of Newcastle-on-Tyne. The OB was a popular choice with small operators in the 1940s and was powered by a smooth-running 72bhp 3.5-litre six-cylinder petrol engine. *Plaxton*

Glasgow and Excelsior European of Bournemouth. Plaxton was no longer a local coachbuilder. It now had customers throughout Britain.

The period at the end of the 1940s and the start of the 1950s saw a revolution in coach design. The typical late-1940s coach differed little in general concept from vehicles built 20 years earlier. While there may have been some significant design developments — such as the widespread adoption of diesel engines for coaches from the mid-1930s — the general layout of a typical full-size coach had stayed the same, with a vertically mounted front engine and the driver sitting alongside it in an enclosed cab.

Left: Plaxton also bodied the standard OB chassis, as seen here on a 1948 coach in the Lincolnshire fleet. It was one of three which had been new to Enterprise of Scunthorpe, a business acquired by Lincolnshire in 1950. *Roy Marshall*

Above: In 1947 Plaxton launched what would turn out to be its definitive body for front-engined chassis. The basic structure was unchanged, but the main pillars were altered so that all were of the same style. Northern Roadways, based in Glasgow, operated this Maudslay Marathon III with Plaxton body. Maudslay was a sister company of AEC, and its coach chassis used AEC engines. The single-piece windscreen was introduced in 1949. *Stephen Barber collection*

Right: Plaxton was also securing sales in the South of England in the 1940s. Two Daimler CVD6s supplied to Rickards of London in 1948/9 carried a discreet Royal Warrant above a small Rickards fleetname. At a time when coaches were painted in light colours Rickards' dark-red livery was unusual.
Roy Marshall

Left: Indicative of the wide range of chassis being bodied in the late 1940s is this Lancet in the fleet of Garelochhead Coach Services, which used an unusual black and white livery. One half-drop window is open for ventilation. The coach carries the name 'Loch Lomond' rather than the operator's fleet-name. All of the company's coaches were named after Scottish lochs. *Harry Hay*

Below left: Foden was one of the pioneers in the use of a false grille to conceal the radiator, on both bus and lorry chassis. The grille incorporated a full-width bonnet, and in an era when virtually all coaches had exposed radiators it added a touch of modernity. This one was photographed in service with Eastern Counties but had been new in 1949 to Clarke's of Felixstowe, whose business Eastern Counties took over in 1951. Around 80 front-engined Fodens were bodied by Plaxton. *Roy Marshall*

Below: Perhaps the most unusual chassis to receive Plaxton's standard postwar coach body were the products of Tilling-Stevens, an old-established manufacturer but one which by this time was a spent force in the coach business. This coach, supplied to N&S of Oadby, Leicestershire, in 1948, shows clearly how the seats rose slightly towards the back, to aid forward vision. The floor under the seats sloped upwards; the gangway, however, was flat. *Plaxton*

Right: Some chassis manufacturers provided a full-width scuttle, which coachbuilders incorporated into their bodywork. These included Seddon, on its small Mark IV chassis — typically a 29-seater at a time when Plaxton's full-size coaches seated 33. Walkers of Slaidburn operated this Mk IV in the early 1960s, it had been supplied new to a Northamptonshire operator. The body is substantially the same as the full-size Plaxton product but less one side window. This coach has semaphore direction indicators, housed in the vertical opening beneath the cab window; these enjoyed popularity in the early 1950s, after which they were superseded by flashing indicators. The four-ringed motif on the radiator indicates the Seddon had a Perkins engine — in this case a 4.7-litre P6. *Roy Marshall*

Right: Morris-Commercial was a short-lived name in coaching, but Plaxton bodied a few chassis in the 1940s. Although at first glance similar to that on the Walkers Seddon, this body has shorter bays, and the same number of side windows as a standard full-size coach. It was operated by Pamal Hire of London. *Roy Marshall*

Right: Commer offered a modified lorry chassis for use as a coach. The Commando had a 4.1-litre six-cylinder petrol engine as used in Humber cars. Looking a bit tired for a coach that was only seven years old, this Plaxton-bodied example is seen in 1954 in service with R. Doughty & Son of King's Lynn. The vehicle visible in the background shows the standard rear-end style for 1940s Plaxton coaches. The area below the rear window incorporated back-lit panels for the operator's name and the registration number. In between there is a central brake light, which could be flanked by optional arrow-shaped direction indicators. *Roy Marshall*

Above: Plaxton's stand at the 1948 Commercial Motor Show at London's Earls Court. On the left is a Commer Avenger for Lingley's Sale-Away Touring Co, based in Sale, Cheshire. The Avenger was a full-size 33-seater, but with an unladen weight of around 5½ tons it was about a ton lighter than rival models from AEC and Leyland. Plaxton would become the major builder of coach bodies on the Avenger, which at this time still used a petrol engine. On the right is a Dennis Lancet III for Brown's of Garelochhead, with that operator's distinctive use of loch names for its coaches — this is *Loch Katrine*. The vehicle just visible between the two coaches in the foreground was a full-fronted Foden for the Scottish Co-operative Wholesale Society's fleet. That all three exhibits came from operators in Scotland and the North of England reflects that Plaxton was at this time still stronger in the north of the country than in the south. *Plaxton*

Left: The Avenger came from Commer with a full-width bonnet, and all Avengers consequently had full-fronted bodywork. New to Ribbeck of Brodick, on the Isle of Arran, in 1950, this one wore its years well when photographed in 1966. *Iain MacGregor*

Right: Parker Motors of Grange-over-Sands used a photograph of a Plaxton-bodied Commer to promote its day and half-day tours in a local guide book – 'A joy and a pleasure, whatever the weather'. However, 'The Latest Luxury Saloon Coaches' was not an entirely accurate description, as this Commer would have been 10 years old when it appeared in the 1959 edition of the local guide. *Stewart J. Brown collection*

Grange & District Red Book 1959

PHONE GRANGE 2623

PARKERS MOTORS LTD.

THE NOOK GARAGE
GRANGE-OVER-SANDS

The Latest Luxury Saloon Coaches

For a Better Tour ride with the RED and GREYS.

Travel by the Red and Grey Coaches for Daily Tours in the Lake District for Comfort and Civility. Starting Point : The Nook Garage, Kents Bank Road. Luxury Saloon Coaches for Private Parties. Special Quotations for Tours Any Distance.

CARS FOR HIRE, DAY or NIGHT.

AUSTIN 6 SEATERS FOR WEDDINGS and STATION ENGAGEMENTS.

Agents for the Provincial Insurance Co

Cars meet Trains by Appointment.

DAY TOURS 9-0 and 10-0 a.m.
HALF-DAY TOURS 2-0 p.m.

Booking Office and Starting Point: THE NOOK GARAGE, Kents Bank Road. Picking up at Grayrigge Hotel.

Agents for Smith's English and Continental Motor Coach Tours.

A Joy and a Pleasure · Whatever the Weather.

Special Day Tours to EDINBURGH during Season—£1/7/0 Return.

But chassis manufacturers were developing a new range of models in which the engine was mounted horizontally under the floor. This exciting development came at the same time as legislation allowing bigger coaches — up to 30ft long and 8ft wide, instead of 27ft 6in long and 7ft 6in wide. Where a typical late-1940s coach seated 33, from the early 1950s the typical seating layout was 41 — almost a 25% increase in capacity, which was a significant benefit for operators.

Plaxton was quick to respond to the challenges which the new underfloor-engined coaches created. First, there was an awareness that front-engined half-cab models were in danger of becoming obsolete almost overnight. The answer to that was to develop bodies with full-width fronts that added a touch of modernity to front-engined coaches and did away with the lop-sided look of the traditional half-cab. Plaxton's full-width fronts were also fitted to existing half-cab coaches by some enterprising operators eager to ensure that their vehicles did not look outdated.

Right: The Foden grille lent itself to full-fronted bodywork, as seen on this 1949 33-seater built for Heeley of New Tupton, Derbyshire. Heeley's business was bought in 1953 by East Midland Motor Services, which continued to run this Foden until 1957. *Roy Marshall*

Left: The brightly named Sunshine Coaches, of Wells, operated this Dennis Lancet, a late example built in 1950 and incorporating the chassis manufacturer's full-width scuttle. It was a 33-seater. *Roy Marshall*

As the switch to underfloor engines created a radical transformation in the appearance of coaches on Britain's roads, a growing number of operators of conventional front-engined models started to specify full-width fronts. Operators had many reasons for continuing to buy front-engined coaches: they were cheaper to buy and to operate, they were easier to work on, not everyone wanted the higher 41-seat capacity of an underfloor-engined model, and, of course, there was a degree of nervousness about new and unproven technology. This 1950 coach for WEMS of Clevedon shows the first standard full front from Plaxton. As on underfloor-engined coaches, only the manufacturer's badge reveals the identity of the chassis, in this case a Crossley. *Roy Marshall*

An alternative version of the full-width front is shown on this 1950 Albion Valiant operated by Greyhound of Arbroath. It had been supplied new to Cotters of Glasgow, which would become a regular Plaxton customer. Behind the fan-shaped moulding it is possible to see that this body has a small rectangular grille not dissimilar to that on the WEMS Crossley. The roof-mounted horns were a Cotters speciality. *Iain MacGregor*

It was at this time that Plaxton started naming its models. The Envoy was a stylish full-fronted body for front-engined chassis, while the Venturer was designed for underfloor-engined models. The Venturer appeared in 1950 and had curved glass corner sections for the windscreens. The entrance was located towards the centre of the coach, meaning that two lucky passengers had a grandstand view of the road ahead from their seats alongside the driver. The option of curved corner glass for the windscreens was also offered on a variation on the Envoy theme, marketed as the Crusader. This was available on both front- and mid-engined chassis.

Some examples of all these body styles had spats to enclose the rear wheel arches. These tended to be short-lived, in part because they restricted the flow of air around the rear brakes, preventing effective dissipation of the heat generated during braking. They soon vanished from Plaxton's options list, although they were to make a re-appearance in the early years of the 21st century on the classically styled 'Grand Tourer' coaches for Wallace Arnold.

The Venturer emerged as the most successful of these models and was built on the two most popular chassis of the time, the AEC Regal IV and Leyland Royal Tiger. The design was also adapted for the popular lightweight Bedford SB.

There was frequent updating of these bodies, with different side mouldings, for example, and from 1951 the availability of glazed cove panels which made the interior brighter.

The 1950s was a transitional decade, for the

Right: The 1951 Envoy body for front-engined chassis was one of the first Plaxton models to be named and was an all-new product. It had deeper side windows, simpler side mouldings, less curvature on the waistline and a new full-width cab. It also had spats over the rear wheels, which while stylish were not very practical, as they reduced the airflow around the rear wheels and could cause the brakes to overheat. Consequently the spats did not stay in place for very long, although they are still *in situ* on this Leyland Tiger operated by Boddy's of Bridlington, seen at Wembley Stadium. Note the air intake above the front windows, a standard Envoy feature.
Stephen Barber collection

Right: Later versions of the Envoy had improved frontal styling with horizontal polished mouldings and the lower front edge of the body built out. Most had simply the manufacturer's badge located above the grille, but on this Foden for Ledgard of Leeds Plaxton has neatly incorporated Foden's own complex mouldings.
R. F. Mack

country, the bus and coach industry and indeed Plaxton. The country saw years of austerity give way to relative affluence as postwar restrictions on the availability of certain products were gradually lifted. Initially this significantly enhanced the company's prospects, but as affluence spread, so the increasing affordability of the motor car started to cast an unstoppable shadow across the industry. By the end of the decade the industry would be in a very different shape from that in which it was at the start.

Coach production was still very much a craft-based business, and Plaxton would build one-offs or modify small batches to meet particular customers' demands. Unusual chassis were bodied, including the mid-engined Atkinson, which had a higher-than-normal version of the Venturer body. A similar body was built in 1952 on the first rear-engined coach to be bodied by Plaxton, a Foden. It would be the best part of 30 years before rear-engined coaches became commonplace. Plaxton also bodied underfloor-engined chassis from Daimler, Dennis and Seddon.

Left: Commer used a Plaxton Envoy to promote its Avenger model in the early 1950s. This advertisement, dating from 1952, describes the coach as 'Silent, safe and speedy'. *Stewart J. Brown collection*

Below: The Crusader was similar to the Envoy but with a more upright front with curved corner sections to the windscreen, which in 1950 was a significant step forward. This Leyland Tiger PS2, new to Blue Bird Coaches of Hull, is seen later in life with Stringers of Pontefract. The side moulding separating the two colours is a later addition, as are the flashing trafficators; when new the coach had semaphore indicators. *Stephen Barber collection*

Right: Buses were not really part of Plaxton's business until the late 1950s, but it did build a few, including the body on this Commer Avenger for Hardwicks of Smainton, near Scarborough. It was a nicely proportioned body, albeit with nothing in common with any other Plaxton products apart from the shape of the glazed name and destination screen panels above the windscreens. *Stephen Barber collection*

Left: There was a Crusader for underfloor-engined chassis which also featured spats for the rear wheels. It was not perhaps Plaxton's most elegant design. This example, on a Leyland Royal Tiger chassis, was for Frostways of Hull. The centrally mounted fog-lamp was an unusual feature. The Crusader was short-lived, output being concentrated in 1951/2. *Stephen Barber collection*

Right: The successful new model was the Venturer, seen here on an AEC Regal IV in service with Strachans of Ballater in the early 1960s. Like most early bodies for underfloor-engined coaches the standard Venturer was a 41-seater. The styling clearly echoed that of the company's late-1940s bodywork on front-engined chassis, even down to the shape of the side mouldings. This coach had been new in 1952 to Broadhead of Dewsbury. *Harry Hay*

Above: The most unusual chassis type to be fitted with a Venturer body was the rear-engined Foden. This was the first rear-engined chassis to be bodied by Plaxton, in 1951. Plaxton bodied six rear-engined Fodens between 1951 and 1958 — after which almost 10 years would elapse before another rear-engined coach was built at Scarborough, on the Dalmler Roadliner. *Plaxton*

Above: There were variations on the Venturer theme, such as this version with a bulbous front end on which the name and destination panels were relocated below the windscreen and the front dome was fitted with tinted glazing. The sidelights are located in heavy mouldings. This body, on a Leyland Royal Tiger chassis, also features top-sliding windows. A step is located above the numberplate and a handle fitted above the Royal Tiger badge to allow the driver to climb up to clean the windscreen; windscreen washers had not yet been invented. The coach is seen in service with Florence Tours of Morecambe. Behind is a Venturer II on a Bedford SB chassis. *Stephen Barber collection*

Right: A Plaxton Venturer forms the centrepiece on this 1950s Valentine's postcard from Gretna Green. Similar cards were produced for other tourist destinations.
Stewart J. Brown collection

Below: A 39-seat Venturer body was fitted to this AEC Regal supplied to Kia Ora Motor Services of Morecambe, which, with sister company Florence Excursions, was a regular buyer of Plaxton-bodied Regals. The coach is seen later in its life with Hulley's of Baslow. The destination display above the front bumper is probably a later addition. *Martin Llewellyn*

Left: These drawings from a contemporary Plaxton brochure show variations on the Venturer theme. The upper, drawn for a Daimler Freeline chassis, has the entrance in mid-wheelbase and uses curved glass on the rear corners; it is shown with optional glazed cove panels. The lower, for an AEC Regal IV or Leyland Royal Tiger, has the entrance immediately behind the front wheel and simpler treatment of the rear glazing. *Plaxton*

The building of bodies on new heavy-duty front-engined chassis came to an end in 1952, although Plaxton would fit new bodies to reconditioned chassis of this layout until the late 1950s. And, of course, bodywork would continue to be fitted to lighter-duty front-engined chassis, most notably the Bedford SB — albeit in decreasing numbers — until the late 1970s.

One operator which went in for chassis rebuilding in a big way was Barton Transport, of Nottingham. In the mid-1950s it embarked on a major programme which saw older chassis lengthened from 27ft 6in to 30ft and fitted with new bodies — Plaxton fitted Venturer bodies to a number of these rebuilds — and would go on from this to become a major supplier to the company.

Pent-up demand for leisure travel, coupled with restrictions on the availability of new cars — not to mention problems with their affordability — saw a boom in coach travel and in coach production in the late 1940s. Established manufacturers like Plaxton struggled to cope with demand, and many small builders appeared, all of which were short-lived and vanished in the early 1950s when the boom turned to bust.

Left: From 1951 the Venturer was made available on the new Bedford SB chassis. This one was operated by Hymas of Burton Leonard, North Yorkshire, and like most early SBs incorporated Bedford's standard grille, beneath which is a tiny Venturer badge. *Roy Marshall*

Right: Throughout the 1950s Plaxton produced alongside its coaches a variety of other types of body. These included fire appliances, as well as vans for the United States Air Force. Closer in spirit to the company's mainstream business was this 12-seat personnel carrier, built in 1953 on a Commer chassis for the Lambton Castle Residential College for Adult Education, in County Durham. The windscreen display promotes the Commer dealer that supplied the vehicle.
Plaxton

Below: For the 1952 Commercial Motor Show the Venturer body was updated with a revised front incorporating a large oval surround for the grille. This is an AEC Reliance operated by Hanson of Huddersfield. The same style of front was introduced on all models.
Martin Llewellyn

As orders for new coaches slowed down Plaxton used its coachbuilding skills to produce other types of bodywork, and from the early 1950s its production lines were also handling fire-engine bodies — including more than 400 of the famous 'Green Goddesses' built for the Ministry of Works. The company also produced mobile canteens and vans for the United States Air Force, for use on its British bases.

A revised Venturer II was unveiled at the 1952 Commercial Motor Show at London's Earl's Court. The front profile was improved with gentle curves, and a new style of grille introduced with a chromium oval surround. This would, in various guises, be a feature on most Plaxton bodies until 1962 and was used on bodywork on the Bedford VAS until 1967. Curved glazing on the rear corners of the body was an option on the Venturer II and was then adopted as standard two years later on the Venturer III, albeit to an improved design.

Early underfloor-engined chassis were heavy. Where a typical 1940s coach weighed less than 7 tons, new coaches in the early 1950s weighed over 8 tons. There soon came an acceptance that the first-generation mid-engined models were over-engineered, and Leyland's Royal Tiger and AEC's Regal IV were replaced by the lighter Tiger Cub and Reliance respectively, shaving more than 1½ tons off the overall weight. This improved fuel economy, which was as much of an issue in the mid-1950s as it would be 50 years later. Plaxton's Venturer body continued with little change on the new lighter chassis.

Left: This is Plaxton's advertisement for the 1952 Commercial Motor Show, as published in *Bus & Coach* magazine. None of the chassis manufacturers mentioned survive, Daimler, Maudslay, Commer and Bedford all disappearing over the following three decades. *Stewart J. Brown collection*

Right: While the bulk of Plaxton's output was of large coaches, the company did build modest numbers of smaller coaches — often using the workshops of the service division rather than having such non-standard products occupying space on the main production line. Seen in the demonstration park at the 1952 Commercial Motor Show at Earl's Court, this scaled-down Venturer for Scott's Greys of Darlington was based on an Austin. Coaches of this style typically carried 14 passengers. *Roy Marshall*

Left: Barton Transport of Nottingham would become a big customer for Plaxton coaches. This 1953 Venturer was built on a Leyland chassis which had been rebuilt by Barton in its own workshops using a combination of new and old parts and was classified by the company as a BTS1/1. Barton rebuilt over 50 older Leylands as BTS1/1 models and had them fitted with new bodies by a variety of builders. An unusual feature is a first-aid kit accessible from outside the vehicle, located in a panel on the emergency door. *Roy Marshall*

Right: Seddon of Oldham played a small part in the supply of coach chassis in the 1950s. This mid-engined model, with Venturer II body, was operated by Hunter of Loanhead. The engine was a vertical Perkins unit. *Harry Hay*

Left and below: In the 1950s a small but growing number of operators were running tours to Continental Europe. Long before the adoption (from the late 1970s) of the so-called Continental door, Plaxton developed a clever step arrangement which allowed passengers to use the emergency exit as a safe means of boarding and alighting in Europe — assuming they possessed reasonable agility. This Venturer II was supplied to Frames' Tours of London in 1955 and was a class winner at that year's British Coach Rally — the first staging of the event, which was held at Clacton-on-Sea. The coach was configured as a 31-seater, and each pair of seats was staggered, the seat nearer the gangway being a few inches further forward than the window seat, to improve the view for gangway-seat passengers. With just 31 seats in a coach designed to hold 38, and with a big six-cylinder petrol engine, this Bedford SB would have been the ultimate in luxury touring in the mid-1950s. *Plaxton*

Right: The Venturer II continued in production on the new generation of lighter mid-engined chassis that were appearing in the mid-1950s. This is an AEC Reliance in the fleet of Cotter of Glasgow. *Stewart J. Brown*

Below: A view of the Kirkby coach dealership at Anston in the 1950s, showing the clever use of the site on an embankment, with a workshop/showroom on two levels. On the upper level, accessible from the petrol-station forecourt, stands a Bedford SB with Venturer II body; the lower level, reached from the area behind the building, houses an unidentifiable coach. Period details include traditional Shell petrol pumps and a rare Austin A90 Atlantic saloon. *Plaxton*

A major change to the Venturer came in 1955 with the introduction of a front-entrance model, which featured an inswing door ahead of the front axle as an alternative to the existing design which had a sliding door behind the axle. To accommodate the entrance a new, more upright front profile was adopted.

The gentle curves of the Venturer, both in the body structure and on the side mouldings, were modified in 1956 with the launch of the Consort. While the basic structure was the same the Consort picked up car styling themes of the time, with the front trafficators incorporated in a chrome-trimmed forward-leaning moulding which resembled the tail-lights of contemporary American cars. There was a similar prominent moulding at the rear. There was a new grille too, and the whole effect was to create a rather flashier look than that of the established Venturer.

Initially the Consort was offered on front-engined Bedford SB and Commer Avenger chassis and on mid-engined models from AEC, Albion and Leyland. Plaxton bodied large numbers of AEC Reliances, but only a small number of Leyland Tiger Cubs and Albion Aberdonians. On mid-engined chassis there was the option of either a centre or a front entrance. There was also flexibility in Plaxton's production, so it was possible to order a Consort-style body but with the more restrained Venturer-style grille and mouldings.

Left: Until 1955 all Plaxton bodies on underfloor-engined chassis were built with centre entrances. That changed with the introduction of an alternative version of the Venturer, with a more upright frontal profile that allowed the entrance to be located ahead of the front axle. This design was offered on a variety of chassis, including the AEC Reliance, Albion Aberdonian, Leyland Tiger Cub and — as seen here — the rare Atkinson Alpha. This coach was new in 1956 to Camplejohn of Darfield but is pictured in the ownership of Yorkshire Traction, which acquired the Camplejohn business in 1961. The glazed front dome was standard on this model. *Roy Marshall*

Below: Production at Seamer Road in 1956. The two vehicles on the left are AEC Reliances with Venturer bodies for Barton Transport. In the centre is a Bedford SB, and on the right a centre-entrance Reliance, both for unidentified buyers. *Plaxton*

Right: A number of operators used Plaxton's front end to modernise outdated half-cab coaches. Although this Bristol L6G coach in the fleet of Dodds of Troon at first glance looks like a Plaxton, it does in fact have bodywork by Burlingham of Blackpool. *Harry Hay*

Below: A shortened version of the Venturer was built on a small number of Albion Nimbuses, and both front- and centre-entrance versions were produced. Dickson's of Dundee opted for the centre-entrance layout; here a Dickson Nimbus pauses in Inverness on a tour to the Isle of Skye. The glazed front dome incorporating a small destination screen was widely used on Plaxton coach bodies in the late 1950s. The Dickson business was purchased by Wallace Arnold in 1963. *Stephen Barber collection*

Above: At the 1956 Commercial Motor Show Plaxton introduced the Consort. On the left is a centre-entrance AEC Reliance for Excelsior European Motorways of Bournemouth, on the right a forward-entrance Reliance for Scott's Greys of Darlington. The Excelsior coach bore a Crossley badge, while the Scott's Greys vehicle was badged as a Maudslay. The third vehicle on the Plaxton stand was a Commer Avenger for Law Bros of Sheffield. Apart from the revised grille, the Consort had different side mouldings to distinguish it further from the Venturer. *Plaxton*

Below: A forward-entrance Consort shows the more upright front end and revised treatment of the side mouldings when compared with the centre-entrance body. This AEC Reliance was operated by Scott's Greys of Darlington. An earlier AEC/Plaxton, also of Scott's Greys, can be seen behind. *Stephen Barber collection*

Above: On Consorts built on front-engined chassis Plaxton dispensed with the lower grille, as seen on a Commer Avenger for Fieldsends of Salford. The lightning flash on the side was an unusual feature for a coach livery in the 1950s, when most operators used liveries which respected the side mouldings on the body. Behind is an older Commer with Plaxton Venturer body, operated by Stringfellows of Wigan. The location is Wembley Stadium. *Stephen Barber collection*

Below: A compact Consort, typically with around 24 seats, was built in small numbers on modified Bedford truck chassis. This one, for Epsom Coaches, is seen at the 1958 British Coach Rally. The gentleman with the top hat was a television personality — Mr Pastry, a character portrayed by actor Richard Hearne — and flagged the first coach away at the start of the rally in Croydon. *Stephen Barber collection*

Although most of Plaxton's output was of full-size coaches it was also able to respond to requests from its customers for smaller vehicles. With the demise of small coach models from Austin, Bedford and Commer at the start of the 1950s there was no obvious choice of chassis, but the company built scaled-down Venturers and Consorts on modified Austin and Bedford truck chassis, albeit in small numbers. Albion introduced a small coach chassis, the Nimbus, in 1955, and Plaxton bodied this too, but again in very small numbers.

By this time Plaxton was established as one of the 'big four' builders of luxury coaches in Britain, the other three being Duple of London, Burlingham of Blackpool and Harrington of Hove.

The company was essentially a builder of coaches rather than buses, although that was about to change. In 1957 Plaxton launched an attractive bus body, the Highway, designed as a 30ft-long 45-seater and most commonly built on AEC Reliance chassis. It proved popular with small operators in the North East of England in particular. When the maximum permitted length of buses and coaches was increased to 36ft, in 1961, Plaxton offered a lengthened version of the Highway, with up to 55 seats.

The Consort was revised in late 1957 as the Consort II and in this form used a grille with an oval surround, continuing a design theme first seen on the Venturer in 1952. The Consort II had deeper side windows and simpler bodyside mouldings.

THREE

Setting New Standards

URING the 1950s Plaxton had been steadily improving its designs. And in 1958 there came a big surprise from the company, when a model which was to revolutionise British coach design appeared at that year's British Coach Rally. This was the Panorama, a breathtakingly different design with an apt and catchy name. What set the Panorama apart from any other coach on Britain's roads was that it had just three big picture windows on each side of the body, achieved by having alternate body pillars stopping at the waist-rail.

The design was developed in conjunction with Sheffield United Tours, which was part of the British Electric Traction group and a major operator of Continental tours at a time when trips

Above: This coach, appropriately named *Panorama Pioneer*, gave Plaxton the edge over its rivals and set new design standards. At various times from the late 1930s Plaxton had used alternate thick and thin pillars to create the illusion of panoramic side windows; in 1958 the illusion was turned into reality, on this AEC Reliance for Sheffield United Tours. The side mouldings, with added polished strips running the length of the coach, were an SUT speciality and were later copied by other operators, while the oval grille surround echoed the style used on the Venturer II. This was a turning-point for Plaxton, setting the scene for a range of Panorama models — and for panoramic-windowed coaches from other manufacturers. Photographed in Scarborough in January 1958, this vehicle went on to win the Coach of the Year award at the British Coach Rally in April. *Plaxton*

by coach to mainland Europe were unusual. SUT took six 36-seat Panoramas on AEC Reliance chassis in 1958, and the vehicle entered in that year's British Coach Rally scooped the 'Coach of the Year' award, following that success with a similar award at the Nice Coach Rally. This was a remarkable coup for a company which was unknown outside Britain, taking part in an event where it faced competition from manufacturers from across Europe.

Above: Continuing changes to the Consort included a new oval grille, curved windscreens and a straighter waist-rail, as seen on this 1960 AEC Reliance for Frames' Tours of London. It was a 43-seater, the maximum number possible in a 30ft-long coach. Most operators preferred to fit 41 seats. *Plaxton*

Right: For the 1959 season the Panorama appeared in production form with a number of changes, the most noticeable being a new, more upright front with an inward-opening door; the prototype had been fitted with a door that opened outwards. The side windows were neater, Plaxton having dispensed with the short window alongside the door, and there was a kink to the waistline at the rear, giving the effect of a tail fin — a styling feature briefly popular on cars around this time. This coach, with SUT-style moulding strips, was new to Hall Bros of South Shields but is seen running for Howletts of Quorn, Leicestershire. *Chris Aston*

The initial Panoramas retained the frontal styling of the Consort II, but by the time of the 1958 Commercial Motor Show in the autumn a revised front with a two-piece curved windscreen was unveiled. This was made possible by a change in the Construction & Use Regulations which dispensed with the requirement to fit an opening driver's windscreen. The curved windscreen was also offered on the Consort body and quickly became a standard feature.

For the 1959 season curved windscreens of what were described as a 'wrap-round' design (borrowing car terminology) were also offered on the Consort IV body fitted to the Bedford SB, a two-piece fixed screen replacing the previous four-piece screen with the mandatory outward-opening section in front of the driver. This improved Consort was also available on the new Thames 570E chassis from Ford, which was a rival to the Bedford SB and would spearhead a growing involvement by Ford in the UK coach business.

Right: A scaled-down version of the Consort IV for Bedford J2S and Commer Karrier chassis was promoted on a postcard distributed by Plaxton. The front showed a side-elevation drawing while the reverse highlighted features such as 'ample passenger room with large seat spacings' and 'perspex panel in front dome, incorporating single destination box, and seven day clock'. The Bedford version was a 16-seater; the Karrier seated 14. *Plaxton*

Below: The Consort was replaced by the Embassy, as seen on a Ford 570E for Harkins of Glasgow. The frontal styling, which had been carried over from the final version of the Consort, might suggest there was little change, but the pillars on the Embassy were angled inwards above the waist; it was only a slight angle, but it did away with the slab-sided look of the Consort and considerably improved the vehicle's appearance. *Iain MacGregor*

An unusual model produced in 1959 was a dual-purpose coach based on an amalgam of the Highway bus with a simplified version of the Consort coach front. These were produced in small numbers on Bedford SB chassis and became known as the Conway, a title never used officially but one by which the model seems to have been best remembered.

The Consort IV was built for two seasons, being replaced by a new model, the Embassy, at the 1960 Commercial Motor Show. Although broadly similar in appearance to the final version of the Consort, the Embassy had an all-new frame in which the pillars were angled slightly inwards above the waist-rail, a relatively small change which made for a considerable improvement in the vehicle's appearance.

The revised pillar profile was also used on the Panorama, which, like the Embassy, had slight curvature on the waistline. The Panorama also acquired a smaller, simpler, grille and quadruple headlights.

Above and left: Most Embassy bodies were built on Bedford SB chassis, like this coach prepared for the 1960 Commercial Motor Show. The interior view shows how bright and airy 1960s coaches could be with glazed cove panels, translucent panels in the roof and net luggage racks to let the light through.
Plaxton

Right: The Atomium, built in Brussels for the 1958 World Fair, has clearly influenced the artist in his choice of background for this 1960 brochure showing a Plaxton coach of the future. *Plaxton*

Coachwork with an eye to the future

Plaxtons

PLAXTONS (SCARBOROUGH) LIMITED
CASTLE WORKS, SEAMER ROAD, SCARBOROUGH
Telephone: Scarborough 6011 (5 lines)

Below: An all-new Panorama appeared in 1961 with a neater grille, and slightly inward-angled pillars as used on the Embassy. The waistline curved slightly towards the rear. The result was a classic design, as seen here on an AEC Reliance operated by Straws of Leicester.
Chris Aston

As the 1960s dawned Britain was on the verge of massive social and technological change, which would gather pace in subsequent decades. These changes would once again have an effect on Plaxton's markets and ultimately on the company itself. Although the effects would prove to be mixed, Plaxton would take full advantage of the opportunities to adapt to new challenges and would conclude the decade in a commanding position.

In 1961 there was a further change in the maximum permissible dimensions of buses and coaches. Length was increased from 30ft to 36ft, and width from 8ft to 8ft 2½in. The first 36ft-long coaches from Plaxton were Panoramas on AEC Reliance chassis in 1961, with Leyland Leopards following in 1962. Bedford introduced a 36ft-long chassis, the twin-steer VAL, in 1962. Plaxton's first body on the VAL was an extended version of the Embassy, with eight small side windows. This was an exhibit at that year's Commercial Motor Show and was rebuilt with the longer side windows of contemporary Panoramas before entering service with World Wide of London. A second, similar Embassy was built on a VAL chassis and had a brief life as a development vehicle for Vauxhall Motors before being sold to Jack Brabham in 1964 for conversion to a transporter for his motor-racing team. These two vehicles were unusual,

although a few similar multi-windowed 36ft bodies were built on AEC Reliance and Leyland Leopard chassis.

When series production of coach bodies on the VAL got underway Plaxton used a version of the Panorama with a large oval Embassy-style grille to ensure an adequate flow of air around the VAL's front-mounted radiator. The VAL could seat up to 52. A similar body was fitted to the new Thames 676E, designed by Ford as a competitor for the VAL but of conventional two-axle layout.

Above: The Panorama had minor variations to suit different chassis. The Dennis Lancet UF had a lower driving position than did other models of the time, which necessitated lowering the windscreen by a few inches. Here a Glenton Tours Lancet, complete with driver in an almost military-style uniform, with buttoned jacket and peaked cap, takes part in the 1961 British Coach Rally at Brighton. This was the last Lancet to be built and thus the last Dennis coach for some 20 years. Glenton operated nine Plaxton-bodied examples. *Stephen Barber collection*

Below: The new Panorama was also available as a 36ft-long coach, which typically increased the seating capacity from 41 to 49 or 51. Provincial of Leicester was the operator of this early 36ft AEC Reliance. *Chris Aston*

Taking advantage of the new limits, the Panorama body on standard AEC and Leyland chassis was increased in length from 30ft to 31ft 10in, allowing more generous legroom for the same number of passengers, usually 41. A small number of Panoramas were built with centre doors, Wallace Arnold and Glenton Tours of London being the best-known users.

The Panorama helped Plaxton secure a growing number of orders from the BET group, whose Sheffield United subsidiary had been closely involved in the original design. BET buyers of the Panorama in the early 1960s included Black &

White Motorways, Midland Red, Ribble and Yorkshire Traction.

There were changes to the Embassy body on Bedford and Ford chassis, and on the diminishing number of Commers being built. The Embassy II, launched in 1962 for the 1963 season, had a distinctive peaked front dome on an otherwise unaltered body. In the autumn of 1963, for the following year, the curious Embassy III was launched, this being a new and distinctive design which adapted contemporary Panorama styling for a front-engined chassis and added a prominent grille, unique to this body.

Plaxton pricing

In 1962 a Panorama body cost £3,925 on a 36ft Leyland or AEC chassis, or £3,475 on a standard-length (31ft 10in) model. Optional extras included:

HMV radio, four speakers and microphone	*£71 0s 0d*
One H.17 heater	*£33 10s 0d*
Formica interior side panels (in place of PVC)	*£25 0s 0d*
Additional 30cu ft side locker	*£35 0s 0d*
Automatic Continental step under emergency door	*£65 0s 0d*
Sorbo rubber floor in lieu of lino	*£52 0s 0d*
Plastic nylon nets to rear of seats (each)	*19s 0d*

new Plaxton Panorama 49-51 seater
on AEC/Leyland II metre chassis

Above: The perspective exaggerated the length of the new model in this rendering of the Panorama body on Plaxton's 1963 brochure. An Embassy II body on a 36ft AEC or Leyland cost £3,875, while the equivalent Panorama was £3,925 — a remarkably small price differential. *Stewart J. Brown collection*

Right: A Plaxton Panorama was used by McDowall's Super Luxury Coaches of Glasgow on the cover and on the centre pages of an early-1960s brochure listing possible itineraries for private-hire clients organising a day out. McDowall's promoted features of the coach, which included 'Air suspension, for floating comfort' and 'Radio so placed to reach all parts without being noisy'. *Stewart J. Brown collection*

McDowall's
Super Luxury Coaches

•

151 RENFIELD STREET,
GLASGOW, C.2.

•

TELEPHONE: DOUGLAS 0883 - 6707

Associated Company | DOIG'S COACHES LIMITED
| 18 INVERKIP STREET, GREENOCK

TELEPHONE: GREENOCK 20571

Left: For operators not wanting the Panorama, all of the improvements in the design were carried over to the Embassy — which was, of course, the same structure but with all the pillars extending the full height of the body. South Wales operator Brewer's owned this attractive AEC Reliance, seen on a private hire at Wembley. *Stephen Barber collection*

Left: A fashionable peak was added to the front dome of the Embassy for the 1962 season and continued through 1963. This could be used to house a small destination display, as seen on this Bedford SB for Don Motor Tours at the 1962 Earl's Court show. Alongside is a Panorama for Sheffield United with wood-grain effect finish on the side — an idea which did not catch on. The third coach is the first Bedford VAL to be bodied by Plaxton, for World Wide Coaches of London. *Plaxton*

Right: The 1963 Panorama had less pronounced curvature on the waist and, on the 36ft-long model, just three main side windows instead of four. This Leyland Leopard was one of a pair supplied to East Midland Motor Services in 1963. It is seen in London 10 years later. *Stewart J. Brown*

Left and above: The World Wide Coaches VAL had a multi-windowed Embassy-style body, with no fewer than eight main side windows, with the centre bay housing the emergency exit. When series production of bodywork on the VAL got underway it was with a standard Panorama-style body, which was generally badged 'Val'. The VAL had a front-mounted engine and ran on 16in wheels — the only 36ft-long coach to do so. It had a front-mounted radiator and so needed the Embassy-style grille to provide adequate cooling. Lofty's of Chester operated the VAL with the whitewall tyres, seen participating in the Blackpool Coach Rally; behind it stands a Panorama body on an AEC Reliance for Fieldsends of Salford. *Plaxton; Stephen Barber collection*

Above left: Although badged as an Embassy the style of body delivered to Wallace Arnold between 1963 and 1966 was really a modified Panorama. Changes included the fitting of top-sliding windows and a centre entrance — a feature by this time rarely specified by British coach operators. *Chris Aston*

Below left: It is hard now to imagine crowds turning out in large numbers to watch a coach rally, but in 1964 it was clearly a big event in Blackpool. The coach being put to the test is a 1964 Embassy III, which was an all-new model with much bigger side windows, making it look more like a Panorama. The model was short-lived: another new Embassy was introduced for 1965. This Bedford SB was owned by Walls of Wigan. *Bedford*

Above: The Highway bus body was made available in the new maximum 36ft length. Whereas most builders of 36ft-long buses opted for different window sizes from those used on established 30ft models, Plaxton retained the existing windows, simply adding more to make up the extra length. The benefit for the operator was standard glass sizes, but the visual effect was of a lot of little windows. Economic of Whitburn operated this 36ft AEC Reliance. *Martin Llewellyn*

Left: Plaxton exported small numbers of vehicles over the years. This unusual dual-door coach combined features from the Embassy and the Panorama and was built in 1964 for Penn Overland Transport in Jamaica. The chassis was also unusual — a front-engined Dodge S350. Similar bodies for Penn were also built on Leyland chassis. *Plaxton*

Left: An alternative moulding arrangement for the Panorama I is seen on another AEC Reliance, operated by Western Welsh. A 38-seater, it was a relatively unusual short version — nominally 32ft — at a time when most Panorama I models were 36ft long. *Stewart J. Brown*

The Embassy III was superseded in the autumn of 1964 by the Embassy IV. This followed the same basic styling but grafted on a new grille, which would appear simultaneously on the Panorama, to produce a body style which would last until the early 1970s. This was done as part of a major redesign of the Panorama, with styling by Ogle Design Associates, a company with which Plaxton worked on various projects over the years. It radically changed the look of the coach, although the actual body structure was unaltered. With the restyle came a new entrance door. The original Panorama had an inward-opening hinged door, and a minor drawback of this design was that as passengers boarded there was the risk of rubbing against the door surface and possibly picking up dirt on their clothes. The Ogle version had a door which pivoted inwards, so that the surface facing passengers as they boarded was the interior rather than the exterior.

The Ogle restyle created two Panoramas. The more striking featured a deep polished moulding below the windscreen which extended the length of the first side window and then swept up the window pillar; this became known as the Panorama I. The alternative design, the Panorama II, had more conventional side mouldings. The Panorama I had fixed side windows and forced-air ventilation, generally with an intake scoop visible on the roof. The Panorama II was usually fitted with top-sliding windows.

Although centre-entrance coaches would continue to be available for a further 17 years the last big order for coaches of this layout was for 21 Ogle-styled Panoramas for Wallace Arnold on AEC Reliance chassis in 1966.

Below: There was even a Panorama I for front-engined chassis, with the broad polished moulding limited to a short piece under the front side window and with the same skirt mouldings as on the standard body for full-size chassis. This is a 1965 Ford 570E operated by Barrie of Balloch. The coach displays the badge of the PVOA (Passenger Vehicle Operators' Association) in the centre of the windscreen. This body was only briefly available on Ford chassis — the 570E being replaced by the new R192 in 1966 — but continued to be offered on the Bedford SB. *Harry Hay*

Above left: The 1965 Plaxton range had styling by Ogle Design, which significantly altered the look of the company's products. Nearest the camera is an Embassy IV on Bedford SB chassis, with just two main side windows and an all-new grille which was carried across all models, as demonstrated by the Panorama alongside. The only carry-over from the previous Embassy model is the windscreen. *Plaxton*

Below left: The Panorama was also dramatically restyled. There were two basic models, although with a lot of flexibility in their specifications. The more striking of the two retained fixed side windows and had a broad polished moulding that swept around the front and underneath the first side window, as shown on an AEC Reliance operated by Sheffield United. This model was known for a time as the Panorama I. *Martin Llewellyn*

Right: The Ogle restyling also produced a Panorama with top-sliding windows, normally offered with this style of moulding and known as the Panorama II. This example, on a Bedford VAM in the fleet of Amos of Belchamp St Paul, Essex, was photographed in the late 1970s but still looks fresh despite being 12 years old. Some operators specified the Panorama II with fixed windows.
Stewart J. Brown

Right: The artist's impression in the brochure for Plaxton's new 1965 models didn't really do justice to the designs, and the nightmarish figure didn't help. This brochure was for the Bedford VAL and listed standard body prices of £4,015 and £4,155, revealing that the Panorama I style carried a price premium of 3.5%. Extras included an HMV radio for £64 and heaters from £36, depending upon how many were required.
Stewart J. Brown collection

There were new chassis designs appearing in the mid-1960s. In 1964 Daimler introduced the rear-engined Roadliner, and in 1965 Bedford launched the VAM, and Ford the R192. Plaxton fitted both coach and bus bodies to the Roadliner, primarily for BET companies, Black & White Motorways taking 38 Roadliners with Plaxton coach bodies between 1966 and 1970, while PMT took 34 with Plaxton bus bodywork (plus three Panorama-bodied coaches) in 1967/8.

The new models from Bedford and Ford had front-mounted engines and set-back front axles which allowed the entrance to be located ahead of the front wheels. The use of truck components kept costs down, making Bedfords and Fords significantly cheaper than models from AEC and Leyland — although with lighter components Bedfords and Fords were acknowledged to be less durable and generally had shorter operating lives.

Leyland also produced a rear-engined chassis, the Panther, a small number of which were fitted with Plaxton Panorama bodies. Plaxton was one of only two builders of coach bodies on the Panther for the UK, and buyers of this rare combination included Seamarks of Luton, Skills of Nottingham and Soudley Valley Coaches of Cinderford.

Below: Plaxton built both bus and coach bodies on the Daimler Roadliner, and here a Roadliner with Panorama body attracts attention at the 1967 Blackpool Coach Rally. It was from the fleet of Black & White Motorways of Cheltenham, a major Roadliner user, and in place of the standard polished metal moulding has twin destination displays and, on the side, the company's name in individual chrome-plated letters. This view also shows the new pivot door, a feature of the models introduced in 1964. *Stewart J. Brown collection*

Right: In 1967 Plaxton secured a handful of export orders for Panorama bodies on the Roadliner, including two for Swiss operators; this coach was for Wittwer of Neuchatel. Early Roadliners such as this had 150bhp 9.6-litre Cummins V6 engines, the first use of a Cummins engine in British buses and coaches. The Cummins engine proved troublesome; later Roadliners used a Perkins V8. *Daimler*

Below: In the 1950s Plaxton had provided front-end structures to allow operators to modernise old half-cab coaches with new full-width fronts. Here the company had provided the front end of the Panorama body as fitted to the Bedford SB to be incorporated into a futuristic vehicle being built by Coventry Steel Caravans for the Ministry of Technology in 1967.
The chassis was, appropriately, an SB. The men in white coats are presumably technologists.
Coventry Steel Caravans

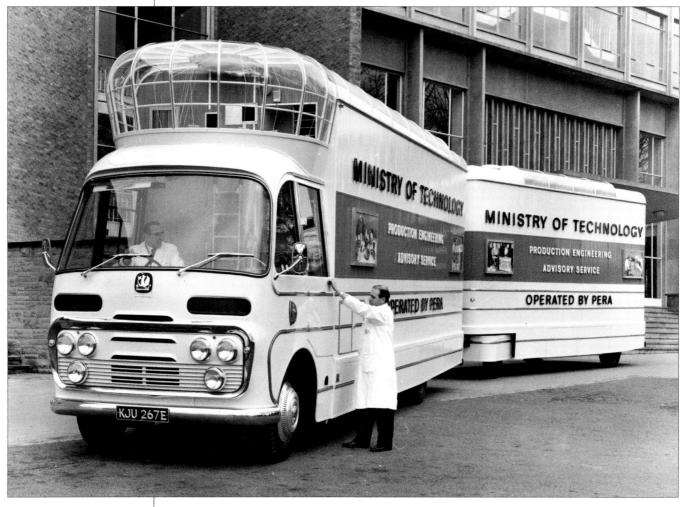

There were changes in the company's bus bodies. In 1962 a new model, the Derwent, was introduced which had an all-metal frame. This was notable in being the first all-metal body built by Plaxton and was also unique in that it was built around frames bought in from an outside company, sufficient parts for 10 vehicles being acquired. The first seven were built on Leyland Leopards for the West Riding Automobile Co. The remaining three would take three years to attract buyers, the last not entering service until 1966. By that stage, a new composite Derwent had been introduced, this having a two-piece BET-style double-curvature windscreen. This was to be Plaxton's first major venture into the bus market and attracted a wide variety of customers during its 16-year production life. Early customers for the new Derwent included West Riding and AA Motor Services, both taking examples on Daimler Roadliner chassis.

There was consolidation in Britain's coach manufacturing businesses in the 1960s. The two smallest mainstream builders disappeared. Blackpool-based Burlingham was taken over by Duple in 1961, while Harrington of Hove withdrew from the market in 1965, Plaxton taking on the responsibility for providing parts support for Harrington coaches. A smaller coachbuilder, Thurgood of Ware, also ceased production in 1965, its premises being taken over by Plaxton and used as southern service centre until 2004.

Above: Leyland used the Panorama on the cover of a 1968 brochure for its Leopard coach chassis.
Stewart J. Brown collection

Left: Plaxton briefly built an all-metal bus body, the Derwent, offered on 36ft-long chassis from Leyland and AEC. It was not a great success, and the composite Highway continued in production. Irvine's of Salsburgh bought a Derwent on AEC Reliance chassis. *Stewart J. Brown*

Right: A new Derwent body, featuring BET-style curved windscreens, was introduced in 1966. This is a Daimler Roadliner operated by AA Motor Services of Ayr. *Stewart J. Brown*

Below: The new composite Derwent body, introduced in 1966, secured some fleet orders, including 20 on Bristol RE chassis for Lancashire United in 1967 that were unusual in being of dual-door layout and in being an amalgam of the Derwent and Highway designs. Although the RE was considered a low-floor chassis at the time, this photograph clearly shows the three-step entrance and exit, with steeper exit steps because the floor was slightly ramped. The use of fixed windows was unusual, ventilation being provided by two lift-up panels in the roof. Fifty similar bodies were supplied to Lancashire United on Seddon RU chassis in 1970/1. *Stewart J. Brown collection*

Above: The Derwent bus body proved to be an ongoing success. This example on a Leyland Leopard was delivered to United Automobile Services in 1967. It had been ordered by Wilkinson's of Sedgefield, which had been taken over by United earlier that year. *Martin Llewellyn / Omnicolour*

Below: Most Derwents were built on Bedford or Ford chassis. Diamond of Stanley took delivery of this Bedford VAM in 1968. *Omnicolour*

FOUR

Coach Market Leadership

HAVING made a major breakthrough in styling with the original Panorama in 1958 Plaxton set another new standard in 1968 with the Panorama Elite. This was a revolution in coach styling — the first British coach to feature side windows with a curved profile, setting standards for coach design for the next two decades. The only items carried over from the previous design were the front grille and the rear light clusters. Viewed from the front, the side profile of the Elite traced a continuous arc of constant radius top to bottom; this was matched by both front and rear panels, which incorporated similar profiles when viewed from the side.

The Panorama Elite was available in lengths of 32ft 6in, 37ft and 39ft 4in, the maximum length for coaches having been increased from 36ft (11m) to 12m in 1968. There was much more steel in the framing of the Panorama Elite than in previous models, as Plaxton slowly moved towards all-metal construction. It was offered on all popular chassis of the day — AEC Reliance, Leyland Leopard, Bristol LH and RE, Ford R-series and Bedford VAM and VAL — and on some less popular ones as well: Daimler Roadliner, Mercedes-Benz O.302, Leyland Panther and Seddon Pennine IV.

On the Bristol chassis, which had a front-mounted radiator, Plaxton was unable to fit its standard destination screen below the windscreen of the Elite, so a modified front dome was devised which incorporated a destination display. This option became known colloquially as the Bristol dome.

By this time only relatively small numbers of traditional front-engined coaches — Bedford SB and VAS models — were entering service, and Plaxton's bodies for these models continued with little change, retaining flat glass side windows.

Left: A scale model of the Panorama Elite produced during its development shows all of the main features of Plaxton's proposed new body. That it has flat glazing and straight pillars is thought to be a reflection of the limits in modelling, rather than any design intention. *Plaxton / Dave Lamb collection*

Below: Trent was a one of a number of BET subsidiaries that were quick to place orders for the new-generation Plaxton coach. This 36ft-long Leyland Leopard is seen in Nottingham when new, in the summer of 1969. The restrained livery adds an air of quality to what was arguably the most stylish coach body on Britain's roads at the end of the 1960s. *Chris Aston*

In 1968 Plaxton's Sales Director, Frank Ford, proposed assembling US-style Flxible buses at Eastfield, and a left-hand-drive demonstrator was brought to Britain, along with assembly jigs from Flxible's factory in Canada. Ford would be remembered as someone with an often radical outlook and is credited with being the driving force behind the movement to take Plaxton to the status of a public company. However, the Flxible project failed, and Ford resigned from the Plaxton board at around the same time.

Also in 1968 Plaxton reached an agreement with a Dublin company, Commercial Sales, which saw Panorama body shells being shipped to Ireland for completion and sale on the Irish market.

As the 1960s drew to a close the transport infrastructure of the country had undergone a major shake-up. The Beeching report had had the effect of dramatically reducing the rail network, and the growth in car ownership was having a detrimental effect on passenger numbers on bus services. In an effort to safeguard public transport the Labour Government under transport secretary Barbara Castle introduced a system of capital grants for buyers of new buses. Introduced in 1968, the so-called 'New Bus Grant' offered operators 25% off the purchase price of a suitable new vehicle (later increased to 50% from 1971). This was to have some unexpected effects on

Plaxton. The aim was to modernise Britain's bus fleet, and the qualifying specifications were based around the requirements of a typical bus for the 1970s — wide entrance, suitability for one-man operation, destination display to the front and a maximum length of 11m. However, a number of enterprising coach operators saw opportunities to benefit from the scheme by adapting a suitable coach design to meet all of these requirements while retaining the style and comfort of a typical touring coach of the period.

An approach was made to Plaxton to adapt the Panorama Elite to include a specification which would qualify for the grant. As long as a vehicle covered a percentage of its annual mileage on local bus services it was eligible. Coach operators soon realised that a qualifying vehicle could spend most of the summer on hires and tours and then cover the necessary bus mileage in the winter.

Charles Marshall was Plaxton's area manager for the North East of England and proposed the idea to a somewhat sceptical senior management. Concerned that the premium position of the company's flagship coach was about to be eroded through being turned into a service bus, they showed some reluctance, but common sense prevailed, and six were built on Leyland Leopard chassis for Silcox of Pembroke Dock, Tyne Valley Coaches, Shaw Bros of Byers Green,

Below: Small operators also bought the Panorama Elite, including Cotter's of Glasgow, a regular customer for Plaxton coaches. This 11m Leopard was a 47-seater which when new in 1969 served as the team coach for Celtic Football Club.
Iain MacGregor

OK Motor Services and Weardale Motor Services, the first vehicles entering service in the summer of 1970.

The resultant model was known as the Elite Express and had a wide two-piece door, a sloping floor towards a slightly lower entrance platform, provision to install ticket equipment, front destination display and a maximum length of 11m. An early customer for the Elite Express was Barton Transport, which took an initial batch of 10 in 1970 on AEC chassis. By 1973 Barton would have bought over 200 Elite Express bodies, marking the biggest renewal of the fleet in the company's history. By 1981 the Barton fleet was 100% Plaxton, and by the end of the Bus Grant scheme in 1984 some 343 new Plaxtons to this specification had entered service with the company.

The Barton investment in bus grant coaches was exceptional, but virtually all operators running bus services and buying coaches specified vehicles which were eligible for the grant; with a 50% rebate of the purchase price it made sound business sense. Of course, the many operators whose business was purely coaching were then disadvantaged, having to pay the full price for their vehicles.

Plaxton's Derwent bus body was also securing regular business. It too qualified for the grant, and was a popular choice on Bedford and Ford chassis as well as on heavier chassis from AEC and Leyland. One of the company's biggest orders thus far in its history came in 1970 when NBC's Midland Red subsidiary ordered 100 Fords with 45-seat Derwent bodies. Other NBC subsidiaries bought smaller numbers of Derwents in the 1970s.

Another big Derwent customer was Lancashire United Transport, which between 1967 and 1976 bought 105, including unusual dual-door examples on Bristol RESL and Seddon RU chassis. Bus production came to a halt in 1977 as demand for coaches was running at an all-time high.

The Elite was a revolution and made the products of Plaxton's only remaining significant competitor, Duple, look old-fashioned. Indeed, Duple responded by recruiting key personnel from Plaxton to produce an Elite look-alike, the Dominant, which appeared in 1972.

At the 1970 Motor Show Plaxton launched the Panorama Elite II, the main change being a tidier front grille. Pantograph windscreen wipers became available as an option. This was followed in 1972 by the Panorama Elite III, which had revised side mouldings and a new tail-light assembly.

Above: The Panorama Elite was built on a wide range of chassis, one of the more unusual being the rear-engined Mercedes-Benz O.302. This was the first Mercedes coach for a British operator and was supplied to World Wide Coaches. It remained unique. *Stewart J. Brown*

Above: The Derwent was also available as a dual-purpose body. In 1971 West Riding took five on Leyland Leopard chassis; fitted with 49 high-backed seats and fixed windows, they were intended for limited-stop services in Yorkshire. Seen in the summer of 1973, this one has strayed somewhat further south as it approaches London's Victoria Coach Station on an express service. *Stewart J. Brown*

Below: The first major change in the Panorama Elite was a revision to the grille, which was reduced in height so that the top was in line with the main bodyside moulding. The moulding strip below the windscreen was lowered a few inches at the same time. The revised model was known as the Panorama Elite II. This coach is unusual in that it incorporates a 1972 Elite II body fitted to a 1962 AEC Reliance chassis. Rebodying was rare by this time, but East Kent had 30 Reliances rebodied by Plaxton in 1972/4. When new they had been fitted with dual-purpose bodywork by Park Royal. *Stewart J. Brown*

A revised body for the Bedford SB and VAS was available from 1972. This had a new front end which incorporated a modified Elite II grille and an Elite III style back end on the straight-sided Panorama body, to produce the Panorama IV.

The standard Elite range was 8ft 2½in wide, but in 1974 a batch of 14 built to a width of just 7ft 6in was supplied to NBC's Greenslades subsidiary for operation in Devon. These were based on Bristol LH6L chassis.

Above: The Elite Express had a slightly wider entrance with a two-piece power-operated door to qualify for the Government's New Bus Grant. Barton Transport bought large numbers and in 1973 alone took delivery of 70 — 40 on Leyland Leopard chassis and 30 on Bedford YRT. This is a YRT. *Stewart J. Brown*

Left: Leyland briefly offered a rear-engined coach chassis, the Panther, alongside its established mid-engined Leopard. Most Panther coaches had Plaxton bodies, exemplified by this Panorama Elite operated by Skill's of Nottingham. The Panther had a front-mounted radiator, and for this Plaxton provided additional ventilation slots. This coach shows what generally became known as the Bristol dome — a roof-mounted destination display that had first been used on bodies fitted to the Bristol RE chassis, which, like the Panther, had a front-mounted radiator. *Stewart J. Brown*

65

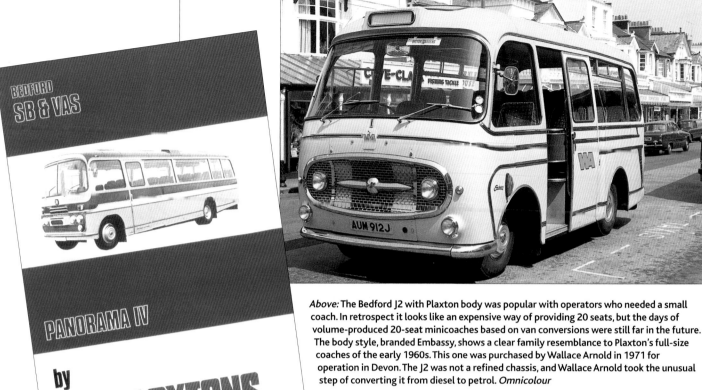

BEDFORD
SB & VAS

PANORAMA IV

by
PLAXTONS

Above: The Bedford J2 with Plaxton body was popular with operators who needed a small coach. In retrospect it looks like an expensive way of providing 20 seats, but the days of volume-produced 20-seat minicoaches based on van conversions were still far in the future. The body style, branded Embassy, shows a clear family resemblance to Plaxton's full-size coaches of the early 1960s. This one was purchased by Wallace Arnold in 1971 for operation in Devon. The J2 was not a refined chassis, and Wallace Arnold took the unusual step of converting it from diesel to petrol. *Omnicolour*

Left: A basic Panorama body with flat glass for the side windows was retained for the Bedford VAS and SB chassis. In its final version, from 1972, it had an Elite-style grille and was known as the Panorama IV. This is a 1974 brochure. *Plaxton*

Below: A Panorama Elite II Express on a Bristol RELH chassis in the Crosville fleet loads in Liverpool for Llandudno. Note the extra cooling slats for the radiator. The rear-engined RE had side lockers as well as a boot for luggage, as evidenced by the driver busy loading passengers' suitcases. *Stewart J. Brown*

Above: The Panorama Elite was launched as the maximum length limit was increased to 12m, and Plaxton had a 12m model in the range right from the start. The extra length meant room for up to eight more seats in a fully seated coach, giving a maximum capacity of 57. A 1973 AEC Reliance operated by Rickards of London is seen in Trafalgar Square. *Stewart J. Brown*

Below: In the early 1970s Seddon had a presence in the coach market with the front-engined Pennine IV. Eight, with Panorama Elite II bodies, were delivered to the SELNEC PTE in 1970, to be followed by eight more in 1971. They had short lives with SELNEC but soon found homes with other operators. *Chris Aston*

Above: This smart 12m-long Panorama Elite, delivered to Heyfordian Coaches in 1975, had 50 seats and a servery. It was based on a Leyland Leopard chassis and carries a 1960s-style Leopard badge. With Continental operation in mind it has a péage window and an additional nearside rear-view mirror. *Plaxton / Dave Lamb collection*

Below: The Bedford Y series was the preferred choice of many coach operators, large and small. Among the larger users was Grey-Green of London. A 53-seat YRT/Panorama Elite II, new in 1974, is seen is on the company's express service from London to Great Yarmouth. *Stewart J. Brown*

The move towards an all-metal structure took a further step forward in 1975 when the Supreme began to replace the Elite. This was recognisably a Plaxton product with curved side windows like the Elite but now extending higher into the roof line. The first Supremes were short versions on the Bedford VAS (Supreme I) and Bristol LHS (Supreme II) and still incorporated some wood in the structure. However, the range quickly extended — literally — to cover full-size chassis. The Supreme was soon offered on full-length AEC, Bedford, Ford, Leyland, Seddon and Volvo chassis. Greater use was made of metal and less of wood, and by the 1978 model year, the Supreme had become an all-steel structure. A Supreme Express was part of the range, meeting the Bus Grant specification, and the distinctive Bristol dome continued as an option.

Production of the Elite III was phased out during 1975, although the final examples were still entering service well into 1976. Curiously the last one didn't enter service until 1988: a solitary Ford R1114 coach had been retained in stock by dealer Jack Hughes for a staggering 12 years, finally being sold to Bob Smith of Sunderland, entering service with an E-prefix registration.

Above: A Bedford Y series — at the time Britain's most popular coach chassis — featured in the brochure used to launch the Supreme. In it Plaxton stated that pre-production models had completed the equivalent of 140,000 miles on tests at the Motor Industry Research Association proving ground. *Plaxton*

Above: The Supreme body looked marginally less attractive on the Bedford VAS because the front-mounted engine dictated the position of the lower edge of the windscreen. However, it was still a pretty little coach and could carry up to 29 people. Shaw's of Barnsley entered this Supreme in the 1979 Blackpool rally. *Stewart J. Brown*

Below: Spruced up ready for the launch of the Supreme at the 1974 Commercial Motor Show is this neat 29-seater on a Bedford VAS chassis. Lettering on the side window indicates that the chassis was priced at £2,373 and the body at £6,206. *Plaxton / Dave Lamb collection*

Above: Outside the 1976 Commercial Motor Show — the last to be held at Earl's Court — Plaxton displayed this small Supreme on a Mercedes-Benz light truck chassis. It was the precursor to the Mini Supreme, which towards the end of the decade would be built on the Mercedes L608D and Bedford CF. *Stewart J. Brown*

Below: More typical of the Supreme range is this 11m model on a Ford R1114 chassis for John Boyce of Glasgow. The coach behind is a Panorama Elite III and illustrates the different style of curvature to the windows: the Elite had a constant-radius curve, whereas the Supreme had pronounced curvature towards the top of the glass. *Stewart J. Brown*

Right: Most full-size Plaxton bodies of the 1970s were built to the maximum permitted width of 8ft 2½in. However, a narrower, 7ft 6in-wide version was available of both the Panorama Elite and the Supreme. On Bristol LH6L chassis it was chosen by NBC for operation over narrow roads in the far South West of England, and in 1979 Western National took six narrow Supreme Express models, with two-piece power doors. The small dark panel below the windscreen could be illuminated to remind passengers to pay the driver when the vehicle was being used on local bus services, on which it was required to complete 50% of its mileage, under the terms of the Government's New Bus Grant. *Stewart J. Brown*

Above: Plaxton made its first sales to the Scottish Bus Group with Supreme bodies on the Seddon Pennine VII, a chassis which had been developed to meet SBG's requirements for a Gardner-engined single-decker. Between 1978 and 1981 Eastern Scottish was supplied with 64 bodies; this is a 1978 Supreme Express, seen leaving Edinburgh's St Andrew Square bus station. *Stewart J. Brown*

By the mid-1970s the chassis market in the UK was changing. In addition to the established UK manufacturers, other commercial vehicle builders in the UK and in Europe were eyeing with envy the buoyant demand, fuelled by the Bus Grant. Volvo was the first overseas chassis manufacturer to make a significant entry, in 1972, Plaxton fitting an early version of the Elite III Express to an 11m B58 chassis for Heyfordian. As the 1973 season progressed Volvo chassis were being bodied for a number of customers, including Parks of Hamilton, Whippet of Fenstanton, Harris of Grays and Skills of Nottingham.

The first Supreme on a DAF, an MB200, was delivered to Robinsons of Appleby in 1976, although it would be 1978 before series production began on MB200s for British operators. The vast majority of DAFs for UK fleets in the late 1970s had Plaxton bodies. From 1976 the company was also successfully exporting Supremes to the Netherlands, on rear-engined DAF SB1605 underframes, and by 1979 it had sold nearly 60.

The export market at this stage was proving to be a promising addition to Plaxton's mainstream business in the UK, and a number of Supremes were being sold in Scandinavia and the Benelux countries on Volvo, Ford and Bedford chassis, and in smaller numbers on Mercedes-Benz and Magirus-Deutz chassis. The success was not sustained, however, and left-hand-drive body production had all but ceased by the end of the decade.

Above: With the Supreme Plaxton secured some export business. A Danish-registered Ford R1114 is seen unloading tourists outside Colchester Castle in 1977. *Stewart J. Brown*

Left: Another Danish customer for the Supreme/Ford combination was Strøby Turistfart, which specified tables in its coach, seen here prior to delivery. *Plaxton / Dave Lamb collection*

Right: The most striking development of the Supreme range was the Viewmaster, Plaxton's first high-floor coach. Although high-floor coaches were becoming common elsewhere in Europe, with this model Plaxton was maintaining its lead in Britain. It was launched in 1976 on the Leyland Leopard, which was a shade underpowered, and then made available on the Volvo B58, where it was more successful. This Volvo B58 with 53-seat body is seen in January 1978, shortly before delivery to Littlewoods of Sheffield. *Stewart J. Brown*

Below: The Supreme IV, introduced in 1978, had a new grille and revised side mouldings. Ellerman Beeline of Hartlepool operated this Ford R1114, one of 24 delivered in 1979 to this company and to the associated Salopia business in Whitchurch. *Stewart J. Brown*

There was growing interest in high-floor coaches of a type often found on the Continent. One of the problems with 12m coaches was that they typically carried eight more people than an 11m — an increase of 16% in passenger capacity — without a commensurate increase in luggage space. This could present difficulties, especially with the growing number of visitors from overseas who often travelled with a lot of luggage. High-floor coaches provided more space for luggage and gave passengers a better view. Plaxton's answer was the Viewmaster — essentially a Supreme with the floor level raised by 12 inches. This appeared in 1976 and marked a radical change to Plaxton's designs, one which was destined to run less than smoothly. The first vehicle was based on a Leyland Leopard chassis for Tatlocks of Radcliffe, whose interest and encouragement were key to the project's progressing. The second vehicle was the first in a batch of 20 for Parks of Hamilton, built on the Volvo B58, and therein lay an unforeseen problem.

All UK coaches have to undergo a static tilt test to ensure their stability in operation, and at the first attempt the B58 failed miserably. An appraisal of the vehicle in question threw up a number of potential solutions, with the primary aim of lowering the centre of gravity. These solutions included moving fuel tanks to a lower position on the chassis, fitting additional fuel tanks and taking all superfluous weight from the upper areas of the body.

The driving position of the Viewmaster was unchanged from that of the conventional Supreme, as was the front panel. The extra height was

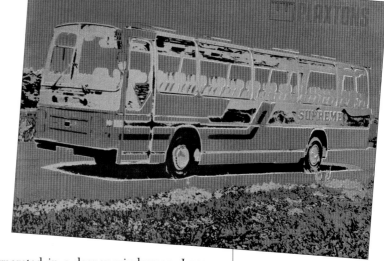

incorporated in a deeper windscreen. Luggage capacity was 11.5cu m (compared with around 6.5cu m on a standard-height coach), and when launched the 12m Viewmaster body cost £19,350, compared with £16,550 for an equivalent Supreme. It was available in both 11m and 12m versions. The 11m model was also offered as an express version, with two-piece doors; most Viewmaster Expresses went to Flights of Birmingham and British Airways. The Viewmaster was also made available on DAF MB chassis, the first going to Youngs of Cambridge.

There were some styling changes to the Supreme, culminating in a revised grille, new windscreens and neater side mouldings in the Supreme IV of 1978. With the exception of the windscreens, these features were carried over to the Viewmaster.

Top: In 1978 the Viewmaster was restyled to match the Supreme IV. Tatlock's of Radcliffe, near Bolton, operated this impressive B58, seen in London outside Westminster Abbey. *Plaxton / Dave Lamb collection*

Above: An eye-catching brochure, with a cover that looks as though it was designed by someone on hallucinogenic drugs, was used to promote the Supreme IV for 1979. *Plaxton*

Right: In the late 1970s a number of Supreme IVs on rear-engined DAF chassis were supplied to operators in the Netherlands. To meet Dutch regulations on turning circles the body was slightly tapered at the front, which meant using a narrower windscreen. *Stewart J. Brown*

Below: The most popular combination for coach operators in Britain in the late 1970s and early 1980s was Bedford/Plaxton, represented here by a YMT operated by Globe of Barnsley and entered, fresh from the factory, at the 1980 Blackpool Coach Rally. It is a Supreme IV, fitted with tables. Visible behind it is another Supreme IV but fitted with the so-called Bristol dome and operated by Bakers of Biddulph. *Stewart J. Brown*

A Supreme GT joined the range in 1980 with a package of 10 items drawn from the options list, offered at a price significantly less than the total cost of the items individually. The specification included laminated windscreens, tinted windows, upgraded heating, stainless-steel wheeltrims, moquette and cord trim on the ceiling, Isringhausen driver's seat and

Blaupunkt audio system. The Supreme GT had a revised grille with thin chrome-plated bars.

Unusual variants of the Supreme and Viewmaster included 12 Supreme bodies on the Mercedes-Benz O.303 for Wahl of London in 1978. These had standard Mercedes front ends and passenger doors, married to the normal Supreme structure. Between 1978 and 1981 Wahl

Above: More adventurous liveries were becoming fashionable from the late 1970s. A particularly striking scheme was used on this Volvo B58 for Limebourne of London. The Plaxton Supreme IV body has the optional Bristol dome. *Stewart J. Brown*

Left: A major upgrade of the Green Line coach network around London was started in 1977, from which year large batches of new coaches were delivered annually. Plaxton secured a fair share of the orders, supplying London Country Bus Services with 60 coaches on AEC Reliance chassis in the years 1977-9, followed between 1980 and 1985 by 15 Leyland Leopards and more than 100 Tigers. Sister NBC subsidiary Southdown was also involved in the network, operating a quartet of Supreme IV-bodied Leopards on the Flightline 777 between Crawley and London via Gatwick Airport. *Stewart J. Brown*

Above: After building one-offs on Mercedes-Benz chassis, Plaxton fulfilled a series of fleet orders placed by Wahl of London for Supreme bodies on the O.303. These coaches incorporated the standard Mercedes-Benz front, including the windscreen, and were noticeably lower-built than standard Supremes on other chassis. *Stewart J. Brown*

Right: Centre-entrance coaches had been abandoned by most operators by the end of the 1950s as they accepted the benefits of having the entrance at the front, where it was under the driver's supervision. The last operator in Britain to buy new centre-entrance coaches was Glenton Tours of London. This is a 1981 Volvo B58 with Supreme IV body. *Stewart J. Brown*

took 31 Plaxton-bodied Mercedes, the first dozen being of two-door layout, to speed boarding and alighting on London sightseeing tours. Plaxton also bodied one left-hand-drive O.303 with a Supreme body which was fitted with two-piece plug doors and was of two-door layout, with the second door in the rear overhang. There were also a small number of centre-entrance Supremes which went to another London operator, Glenton Tours. Glenton took Supremes of this layout on AEC Reliance, Leyland Leopard and Volvo B58 chassis until 1981, which was fully 20 years after centre entrances had been considered obsolete by most coach operators. A one-off Viewmaster was built on a Magirus-Deutz chassis for an operator in Denmark.

The 1970s had been good years for Plaxton, with annual output often topping the 1,000 mark — well ahead of Duple, its nearest competitor. Sales reached a peak in 1979, when more than 1,300 new Plaxton coaches entered service in Britain.

As the Supreme neared the end of its production life Plaxton added new models and options. This was in 1981, and the new models were the Supreme V and VI. There was a completely new rear end with a much shallower window and bigger tail lights, the latter giving a clue as to what

was coming on the Supreme's replacement. The Supreme V was essentially a replacement for the Supreme IV, while the Supreme VI was dramatically different, with much shallower side windows which used flat glass and were double-glazed as standard. This was a response to Duple's Dominant III, which featured shallow trapezoidal windows to give the effect of forward-sloping pillars. It was one of the few occasions where Duple was ahead of Plaxton in terms of design, and Plaxton's Supreme VI lacked the confidence of the Duple design. Comparatively few were built. In 1982 the range — which still included the GT — was promoted as the Jubilee Supreme to mark the company's 75th anniversary.

As well as building bigger coaches — the Viewmaster — Plaxton was still producing small numbers of small coaches, usually built by the service division rather than on the main production lines which were not set up to handle such distinctly different vehicles.

Whilst much attention was being paid to Plaxton's largest coaches, those at the opposite end of the scale were not being ignored. The Supreme I was still available on the Bedford VAS (by now known as the PJK) and the Bristol LHS still had the equivalent Supreme II body.

Above: **Perhaps the least attractive version of the Supreme, with shallow, flat-glass windows, was the Supreme VI, built in small numbers in 1981/2. The livery application used by Atkinsons of Ingleby Arncliffe, North Yorkshire, on this Ford R1114, with a dark area above the windows, flattered the design. The coach is seen at the 1982 Blackpool Coach Rally.** *Stewart J. Brown*

Above: The Mini Supreme on the Bedford CF was an unusual-looking coach and was built by Plaxton's Service Division. It seated 17. This example for Shearings Ribblesdale is posed for comparison alongside a Supreme IV GT. *Plaxton*

Right: Shearings also took Mini Supremes on Mercedes-Benz chassis. The body was better proportioned on the bigger chassis. *Plaxton*

Left: Among the designs being produced by Reeve Burgess when the company was taken over by Plaxton was the Reebur 17 minicoach, built on Ford Transit and Bedford CF chassis. It had crisp lines and, although quaint now, was not unattractive by the standards of the day. Strathmartine Coaches of Dundee purchased thIs Transit in 1980.
Stewart J. Brown

Both were updated to Supreme IV standard in 1979. On an even smaller scale, territory alien to Plaxton since the end of production of the 18-20 seat Embassy IV on the Bedford J2 in 1971, the service division built 41 Mini Supremes — essentially a scaled-down version of the full-sized coach — between 1979 and 1982. There were 35 17-seaters on Bedford CF chassis and six larger 25-seaters on Merccdes-Benz L608D. Most went to small operators looking for a minicoach which offered more comfort than a van conversion, although a number of Bedfords and Mercedes were bought by tour operator Shearings for use on feeder services.

These were small numbers, but Plaxton was about to get into small vehicles in a big way. In 1980 it acquired Reeve Burgess, a company which was based in Pilsley, south of Chesterfield, which built small buses and also did other types of bodywork including crew-cab conversions of trucks. In 1976 the company had launched a purpose-built minicoach body, the Reebur 17, on Bedford CF chassis. The '17' referred to the seating capacity, and the angular but attractive Reebur body was also offered on the Ford Transit. A bigger Reeve Burgess coach, the RB26, on an MAN-VW 8.136 chassis, was introduced as Plaxton took the company over, and this was developed into the Riviera. It remained in production until 1988 but was built only in small numbers. Four Riviera-style bodies were built on

unusual 10m Leyland Tiger chassis for Tayside Transport in 1986.

Plaxton re-entered the bus market in 1980 with a new all-metal body, the Bustler. This had a fairly high waistline and a shallow cantrail, and hinted at the next stage in Plaxton's coach designs. It was built on a range of popular chassis, starting with the Bedford YMT, a model popular with small fleets, and later appearing on other models, including the Leyland Leopard, Ford R-series and Volvo B10M. Some Bustlers were built with centre doors on both sides of the body for use on airport transfer work at Heathrow. The Bustler was also offered on Dennis chassis, but none was built.

In 1981 a new chassis manufacturer appeared in West Yorkshire — Ward. The company was in fact a coach operator, and it turned to Plaxton to body its first chassis, the Dalesman. This was fitted with a standard Supreme body in 1982. Plaxton bodied another six Wards in 1983/4 before the company gave up on chassis production.

RB 26 Midi Coach   REEVE BURGESS

The new RB26 from Reeve Burgess, designed and manufactured to satisfy the most stringent demands of the coach operator.

Based on the new M.A.N.-VW 8.136 chassis capable of displaying levels of performance and reliability previously unknown in the midi coach class.

A superb example of co-operation between coach builder and chassis manufacturer culminating in a coach of outstanding quality.

Above: The RB26 was a 7.75m-long 26-seat coach built by Reeve Burgess on the MAN-VW 8.136 chassis, powered by a 136bhp 5.7-litre MAN engine. The front would be restyled under Plaxton ownership, using curved windscreens and a new glass-fibre moulding to create the Riviera. *Plaxton*

Above: Launched in 1980, the Bustler was available on a range of chassis. One of the biggest orders came from Ralph's Coaches for a contract at London's Heathrow Airport; in 1981 it took 26 on Ford R1014 chassis, of which 14 were three-door 29-seaters.
Stewart J. Brown

Right: Plaxton exported Bustlers in kit form to the Philippines. One customer was Viron Transit, which took this rear-engined Hino. Sliding flat-glass side windows were fitted — with a heavy tint. Note the Plaxton sticker in the destination box.
Plaxton

Left: Plaxton kits were also used to build coaches in the Philippines. The Supreme-style windscreens are the only recognisable Plaxton feature on this rear-engined MAN for Pantranco. The vehicle has more generous ground clearance than standard Plaxton products, to cope with rough roads. The kits were assembled by Manila Motor Works. *Plaxton*

Left: Another unusual chassis to be bodied by Plaxton was the Ward Dalesman. This is the first, on show at the British Coach Rally at Brighton in 1981. It had a mid-mounted Perkins engine. *Stewart J. Brown*

FIVE

The Paramount Years

In 1982 Plaxton replaced the Supreme with the Paramount, which used shallower windows and square-cornered rubber mounting for the glass. This was the original 3200 model. Note the short 'feature' window. *Plaxton*

THE start of the 1980s had been marked by the biggest single change to coaching in the UK since the Road Traffic Act of 1930, which had placed with the Traffic Commissioners the responsibility for licensing any operator wishing to run regular bus or coach services. These licences became highly prized, and, as most were held by big operators, the number of independents who had the right to operate coach services was relatively small. The newly elected Conservative Government had a radical agenda of de-regulation across industry in general, and road transport was no exception. The first step towards this was the removal of all regulation on long-distance coach services (longer than 56km) in 1980.

The effect of this was an explosion in express coach services from operators not previously involved, as well as expansion of services by existing National Bus Company and Scottish Bus Group companies. Newcomers included Stagecoach and the British Coachways consortium.

Competition became the order of the day. With widening choice, the opportunities for price as a differentiating factor were limited, and other features had to come into the equation — levels of service, convenience and ultimately the standards and facilities of the vehicles themselves.

Operators were seeking new and distinctive products. At first, vehicles from Continental European manufacturers provided an answer, but at home Plaxton was addressing the market's

needs with plans for a radical new design. In 1982 the company unveiled a new range: the Paramount. This was designed from the outset to include a high-floor model. The Paramount 3200 replaced the Supreme, while the 3500 replaced the Viewmaster, the figures indicating the nominal body height in millimetres.

The Paramount had a steel frame. The main bodyside panel was a single sheet of Zintec-coated steel stretched over the frame; previous Plaxton models had used aluminium side panels. A single-piece windscreen was standard on the 3200, a horizontally split screen on the 3500. Twin radial arm wipers were an option across the range. Operators requiring destination equipment — primarily NBC, the Scottish Bus Group and those needing specifications which met the Bus Grant requirements — got a three-piece screen, with the destination display located behind the upper glass panel and pantograph wipers on the split lower screens. The whole design was much crisper than the Supreme. The waistline sloped forward at the front, and there was a short window bay — generally described as a 'feature window' — just aft of the front wheel arch.

Left: A pre-launch brochure for the Paramount 3200 with an artist's impression of the completed coach. It was listed in four lengths — 8, 10, 11 and 12m — on five chassis — Bedford, DAF, Ford, Leyland and Volvo. The company also had no fewer than 13 dealers at this time. *Plaxton*

Below: To support the Paramount Plaxton offered a range of standard livery layouts, some of which proved popular with customers, such as schemes 2 and 3. This copied a similar arrangement developed by the company's biggest rival, Duple. *Plaxton*

Right: Harry Shaw of Coventry was an early Paramount customer, taking two on Leyland Tiger chassis in 1983, including this 57-seater seen on an excursion to Weston-super-Mare, a popular destination for day trippers from the West Midlands. The raised roof ventilators suggest a warm day. Air-conditioning was not yet common on coaches in the 1980s. *Stewart J. Brown*

Below: The Paramount won new customers for Plaxton, including Scottish Bus Group subsidiary Western Scottish, which took eight 3200 bodies on Dennis Dorchester chassis in 1983. The windscreen is in three sections, with the destination set behind the top section. For these vehicles Western abandoned its traditional livery layout and specified one of Plaxton's standard schemes. It placed repeat orders for the Dennis/Plaxton combination but this time opted for the high-floor 3500. *Stewart J. Brown*

Borrowing from contemporary motor industry practice, Plaxton launched the Paramount with a range of standard specification packages. These had star ratings, from one to four stars, each offering more equipment. The one-star package, for example, included a Radiomobile cassette player and stainless-steel wheeltrims. With two stars came reclining seats and a better quality radio/cassette player from Blaupunkt. Three stars added double-glazing and features to comply with Germany's Tempo 100 rules, which allowed coaches to operate at speeds of up to 100km/h on the autobahn. The four-star package added a toilet and a Continental door.

As an indication of the costs involved, when it was launched a basic Paramount 3500 body on a 12m chassis cost £35,985. With a one-star package this rose to £36,925; a two-star package cost £41,665, a three-star package was £46,145, and the comprehensive four-star package cost £49,145. It was a bold idea, but the nature of the coach industry was such that operators often wanted different combinations of features from those which Plaxton had packaged together. So while the star ratings might have been a starting point for operators working out a specification, there were still other options which had to be incorporated.

The Paramount 3200 was built in lengths of 8, 10, 11 and 12m and at the time of its introduction was available on suitable chassis from Bedford, Dennis, Ford, Leyland, DAF, Scania, Volvo and Ward Bros. The 3500 was built only as an 11 or 12m coach on heavy-duty chassis — initially on Leyland, Dennis, DAF, Scania and Volvo. Plans were announced in 1985 to sell Paramount-bodied DAFs in Holland, building on the success of Supreme sales in the 1970s, but these did not proceed.

The Paramount was a popular body. It was bought in large numbers by NBC, and could be seen on National Express services and on London Country's Green Line network. It was bought by the Scottish Bus Group for express services and touring. Most Paramounts for NBC and SBG were on Leyland Tiger chassis, but SBG's Paramounts included 23 on the Dennis Dorchester. A small number of Dorchesters were fitted with Paramount bodies for other operators, including Bullock of Cheadle, and for three public-sector operators, namely South Yorkshire PTE and the municipal fleets at Leicester and Kingston-upon-Hull. Plaxton also fitted Paramount 3500 bodies to Leyland's short-lived Royal Tiger rear-engined underframe.

Above: **The Plaxton Paramount 3200 on Leyland Tiger chassis was added in large numbers to the London Country fleet, primarily for the Green Line network. There were 40 11m and 20 12m Tigers delivered in the winter of 1983/4, and these were followed by 15 11m and 20 12m models early in 1985. An 11m coach leaves Victoria Coach Station for Oxford in 1987. Like the vehicles for SBG, most Paramounts for NBC had destination blinds.** *Stewart J. Brown*

In 1984 Plaxton built its first-ever double-decker, the Paramount 4000. This was built to an overall height of 4m — the accepted European standard for double-deckers — and it was based on a three-axle Neoplan underframe. A typical Paramount 4000 seated 71, but the design could accommodate up to 81 people if specified without a toilet. The first was built for long-standing Plaxton customer Excelsior of Bournemouth and was followed by others for NBC, which took 27 in the years 1984-6, most for use on busy National Express 'Rapide' services.

From 1985 the Paramount 4000 was in addition offered on Scania K112TR chassis, London operator Grey-Green being one of the first users. This was soon followed by a version for the mid-engined Volvo B10MT, the Paramount 4000RS — the letters indicating Rear Saloon. The first of these went to a Scottish operator of long-distance coach services, Newton of Dingwall. These seated 64, with 55 seats in the main saloon and nine in the small area behind the rear axle, and offered a generous 13.4cu m of luggage space.

Availability of the Paramount 4000 was extended to DAF chassis in 1987, using the rear-engined SBR3000. The last double-deckers were built in 1990 on Volvo B10MT chassis for

operation on the network of airport services run by Flights of Birmingham, on which they each covered between 80,000 and 100,000 miles a year. In all just under 100 of the 4000-series models were produced — 30 Neoplans, 24 DAFs, 23 Volvos and 22 Scanias. All were of three-axle layout, necessary to cope with the added weight of the 4m-high body.

The mid-1980s saw a short-lived interest in coaches with a low driving position. The only real benefit was that the passengers seated immediately behind the driver got a better view forward. A major drawback was that the driver had a less commanding view of the road ahead.

The first low-driving position coaches built by Plaxton, in 1984, were unusual in that they were on chassis built by Quest Chassis Developments, a Midlands-based business which tried, unsuccessfully, to break into the bus and coach market. Excelsior of Bournemouth (unwisely, as it transpired) ordered 25 chassis from Quest, with an uprated marine version of the six-cylinder Ford 360T engine which had powered several generations of Plaxton-bodied Ford coaches for Excelsior. These were known as the Quest 80 VM — the letters being the initials of Excelsior owner Vernon Maitland.

Above: The most striking version of the new Paramount range was the 4000, Plaxton's first double-decker, which was added in 1984. The first version was built on a Neoplan underframe, and Plaxton supplied 27 to NBC in the years 1984-6. Here a Yorkshire Traction example loads in Sheffield for London.
Stewart J. Brown

Left: In 1984 Plaxton worked closely with DAF in the UK launch of the middleweight SB2300 and so doing enlisted the help of prize-winning middleweight boxer Alan Minter. This picture shows him with the Plaxton sales team of the day. From left to right they are Dick James, Steve Pickup, Geoff Hughes, John Birley — then comes Alan Minter — followed by David Goodare, Maurice Bateman and Bob Walmsley.
Courtesy Bob Walmsley

It soon became apparent that the Quest 80 was not quite as well engineered as it should have been, and in an unusual — indeed, perhaps unique — development the troubles experienced by Excelsior with the first deliveries were enough to call a halt to production before all 25 had been completed. The 17 that were delivered had short lives with Excelsior. Of the eight remaining chassis in the order, four did reach Excelsior but only to be used as a source of spares, and two were bodied by other body-builders and ultimately exported to Cyprus. Plaxton had no further dealings with Quest and the business ceased manufacturing in 1985.

In January 1985 the first major revisions to the successful Paramount range were unveiled. The Mk II had a revised interior, a new entrance door, a neater grille, new wheeltrims and continuous side mouldings below the windows which bridged the gap which had been left under the feature window on the original model. Bonded glazing was offered as an option. The Mk II was available on chassis with low driving positions, in which case it was the 3200LS or 3500LS — the letters indicating low screen.

Also new in 1985 was the introduction of the Mercedes-Benz O.303 chassis, pioneered by Yeates, the Loughborough-based Plaxton dealer following their appointment as Mercedes-Benz agents. The O.303/Paramount was reputedly the most expensive British-bodied coach available at the time. When it appeared at the 1985 NEC Show, Dennis Brown, a well-known and long-serving salesman for Yeates, lavished praise on the vehicle as he demonstrated its features to one potential buyer. 'It would be your flagship,' he suggested to the operator. 'Flagship?' replied the startled customer. 'Battleship, more like — it'd just about sink me!' This particular vehicle was to remain unique, although Mercedes would come back into the Plaxton portfolio a few years later.

It took sharp eyes to spot the difference between the original and Mk II Paramounts, and the updated model was to be short-lived. At the 1986 Motor Show Plaxton launched the distinctively different Paramount Mk III, which featured a completely revised window line, bonded glazing as standard, and new front and rear panels. Bonded glazing was becoming increasingly common on European coach bodies, and it offered a neater appearance and a slight reduction in weight as well as contributing to the overall strength of the body. On the Mk III Plaxton abandoned the short feature window, and instead adopted a step in the waistline over the front axle. Low-driver versions continued to be available. Styling was by Ogle. It would receive a slight revision in 1988, when matt-black trim replaced polished finishes on the exterior of the body.

Left: A batch of Paramount 3200s on rear-engined Quest 80 VM chassis for Excelsior of Bournemouth had low driving positions and deep windscreens, anticipating the 3200LS, which would be offered on other chassis with low driving positions; the windscreen was that used on the standard Paramount 3500. The Excelsior coaches also lacked the feature window. Two Quests head out of Parliament Square, London, in 1984. *Stewart J. Brown*

Below: The Paramount III had a new gille as well as a step in the waist where the feature window had previously been fitted. This 1987 delivery to Lowland Scottish, on Leyland Tiger chassis, was a 50-seater with toilet, for operation on Scottish Citylink express services. *Stewart J. Brown*

Above: The low-driver version of the Paramount III was relatively uncommon, as operators were reverting to coaches with standard driving positions. Shearings took delivery of 25 low-driver Leyland Tigers in 1987 with 3200LS bodies, some of which were in National Holidays livery. *Stewart J. Brown*

Right: While most Paramounts were built on Volvo chassis, there were significant numbers built on other makes. This is a Scania operated by Paramount Leisure — part of PMT, hence the prominent red lettering in the 'ParaMounT' name on the side of the coach, a K112. *Stewart J. Brown*

Unusual Paramounts included a one-off on a Bedford VAS for Stewarts of Dalavich in 1986 and four 7ft 8½in-wide 10m Paramount IIs which were used to rebody 10-year-old Leyland Leopards for Wallace Arnold in 1987. All of these non-standard bodies were built by the service division.

Plaxton was on the verge of major change. At the end of 1986 it purchased the Kirkby group for £8.5 million. Kirkby was a major coach dealer, based at Anston, near Sheffield, and it also had a number of car and van dealerships across the north of England. It would soon be the Kirkby management which was in the driving seat at Plaxton.

One outward sign of change was the abandonment of the castle logo which had been used intermittently over the years. In its place came a stylised bird partially enclosed by a circle. The bird — officially an arctic tern, unofficially the Plaxton budgie — was intended to conjure up images of freedom of movement. The bird logo would be used as a badge on the company's bodies from 1991.

With a standardised range Plaxton was able to operate more efficiently, and with more investment in its plant at Eastfield the Seamer Road factory became redundant in 1988, production thereafter being concentrated on one site. This eliminated the need to move part-built vehicles between the two sites, an expensive and time-consuming process. The Seamer Road site now houses a retail park. A showroom was erected at the entrance to the Eastfield factory in 1990.

The unsuccessful Ward chassis business re-emerged as ACE — Alternative Chassis Engineering — under different ownership, but this project was no more successful. Plaxton bodied five ACE Puma midi-sized chassis with 35-seat versions of the Paramount 3200 body in 1985/6, before ACE closed down.

More significant closures among chassis makers in the mid-1980s involved the two leading lightweight manufacturers. Ford withdrew from the coach market in 1985, followed by Bedford in

L.F. STEWART & SON

1987. Plaxton had been bodying Bedfords since the 1930s, and Fords since 1959.

Yet as these established manufacturers were making an exit from the coach business Dennis was looking at strengthening its position, and this it did with the Cummins-powered Javelin, announced in 1987. Plaxton would be the major builder of bodywork on the Javelin, which had the engine mounted just ahead of the rear axle, which meant there was space for luggage lockers under the floor, ahead of the engine, as well as in the conventional rear locker. Javelins were initially fitted with Paramount 3200 bodies.

By the late 1980s National Express was firmly established as the leading operator of express coach services in England and Wales. It did not as a rule run its own coaches, instead contracting its services out to other operators which provided coaches to National Express's specifications. In an endeavour to ensure uniform high standards National Express teamed up with the leading body-builder, Plaxton, and the leading chassis supplier, Volvo, to create a standard coach — the Expressliner — which it strongly encouraged its contractors to specify.

Launched in March 1989, the Expressliner was based on the Paramount 3500, and its specification was developed in conjunction with National Express and a number of its contracted operators. Two basic variants were offered, one for conventional express routes and one for the higher-quality 'Rapide' operation. Both had an unglazed rear end with a large National Express 'double-N' logo moulded in to the upper section of the panel. 'Rapide' vehicles seated 44 or 46 and had a full servery for on-board catering. Conventional vehicles replaced this with an additional three seats.

Relatively unusual though the specifications were at the time, the most radical aspect of this project lay in the way in which the vehicles would be supplied. Plaxton, Volvo, Lombard (the finance arm of NatWest Bank) and National Express entered into an arrangement whereby the vehicles would be leased from National Expressliners, a new company owned jointly by Roadlease (Plaxton's commercial finance division) and Lombard. Maintenance costs would be included in the contract, carried out either by Volvo dealers or the operators themselves, and the lease would be linked to the award of an operating contract from National Express.

Ultimately the aim was to make the use of Expressliners compulsory for all operators of National Express routes. As their contracts came up for renewal, they would be awarded normally for a five-year period on condition that a new Expressliner was sourced from National Expressliners for the same period. There were safeguards for the operator such that in the event

of a contract being terminated prematurely (as a result of network changes, for instance) the vehicle could be returned if no suitable alternative work could be allocated to the operator. At the end of the contract the intention would be to award it to the same or a different contractor with another new vehicle. This appeared to have a double benefit for Plaxton: a new coach would be sold with each new contract, and when the contract ended Plaxton received the vehicle back, ready for refurbishment and resale, thus maintaining a supply of good-quality used coaches for the Kirkby dealership.

Although the major benefit would be to National Express passengers who could be sure of a consistent level of service across the entire network regardless of who operated the vehicles, it soon became apparent that the idea was not universally popular. There was resistance from operators, many of whom felt they were being railroaded into taking on a commitment for funding and maintenance of vehicles which their experience told them they could provide more efficiently by other means. Vehicle leasing was a popular practice in the industry, but contract

Above: To raise quality on National Express services Plaxton, Volvo and the Kirkby dealership worked with National Express to develop a standard-specification coach based on the Volvo B10M, with Paramount 3500 bodywork incorporating a destination display and a solid rear panel with an embossed 'double-N' logo. The package was marketed as the Expressliner. This 1990 coach shows the revised grille fitted to later Paramount IIIs. *Plaxton*

maintenance was less common, and many companies still preferred to buy vehicles outright. Of
more than 200 Expressliners which entered
service between April 1989 and the cessation of
Paramount Expressliner production in the middle
of 1991 only a handful were to be replaced with
vehicles on the same basis. The real sting in the
tail for Plaxton came with the flood of vehicles
returning at the end of their leases between 1994
and 1997, at a time when demand for used
coaches was low.

Throughout the 1980s buses were still a
relatively small part of Plaxton's business. A new
Derwent body went into production at the end of
1986 to replace the 1980 Bustler model. The first
Derwents were built on Bedford YMT chassis, but
the body would later be made available on the
Volvo B10M — the first was at the 1987 Coach &
Bus show, promoted as the Derwent 3000. Other
chassis fitted with Derwent bodies included the
Leyland Tiger, and the rear-engined Scania K93, a
batch of 10 being built in 1989. From 1990
the Derwent was offered on the Dennis Javelin,
the first of these going to Eastern Counties.
Large numbers of Derwents were built for the
Ministry of Defence on Leyland Tiger chassis.

In 1988 Plaxton made a surprise move, buying
French coach manufacturer Carosserie Lorraine

from Iveco. The deal was completed just weeks
before the 1988 Coach & Bus show, and in the
demonstration park Plaxton had a Carosserie
Lorraine product, a neat left-hand-drive 28-seat
midicoach based on a rear-engined Iveco 315,
which was being exhibited to gauge reaction
from operators.

The reaction was good enough for Plaxton to
commission a batch of 12 right-hand-drive
coaches for 1990, with the first being on the
company's stand at the 1989 show. This was a
33-seater with a 168bhp 5.5-litre engine and a
ZF S6-36 gearbox — an attractive package.

Over the years Plaxton had bodied small
numbers of Mercedes-Benz chassis, starting with
a single O.302 in 1968 which was purchased by
World Wide Coaches of London. There was
another O.302 in 1974, for Blueways of London.
After batches built for Wahl between 1978 and
1981 came the aforementioned one-off Mk II
Paramount 3500 on an O.303, which appeared at
the 1985 British Coach Rally at Brighton and was
ultimately bought by Deeble of Liskeard. But in
the spring of 1989 Plaxton announced that it
would offer bodywork on the O.303 as part of its
mainstream product range. The first was unveiled
in 1990, and with a 290bhp V8 engine it was
a powerful coach by the standards of the day.

Left: Lothian Region Transport
was among the diminishing
number of operators that
specified Leyland Tiger chassis
at the start of the 1990s.
This 53-seat Paramount III
entered service in 1991.
Plaxton

A batch of 25 was built, buyers including The King's Ferry (the biggest user, with eight), Wallace Arnold and Shearings.

In the summer of 1989 there came what would prove to be a pivotal event in Plaxton's history: the purchase of Henlys. Primarily a car sales business, it also owned specialist coachbuilders Mellor and limousine manufacturer Coleman Milne. The group adopted the Henlys name, although individual companies and their names — Plaxton, Kirkby and Reeve Burgess — were retained.

In terms of coach dealing, one of Kirkby's main rivals, London-based Arlington, decided to withdraw from coach sales in the autumn of 1989. Kirkby acquired Arlington's stock of new and used vehicles, consolidating the company's position as one of Britain's biggest specialist coach dealers. Arlington, of course, had been Plaxton dealers since the late 1930s. At the start of 1990 Kirkby was renamed Plaxton Coach Sales, although in 1991 it reverted to the Kirkby Coach & Bus name.

Right: The final version of the Derwent was built on a range of chassis, the body height varying according to the chassis on which it was built. The tallest Derwents were on Dennis Javelin chassis, as seen here with Eastern Counties which took 10 51-seaters in 1990. *Dennis*

Below: The Derwent looked better on lower-framed chassis such as the Volvo B10M. This was one of a pair for Scottish operator Whitelaw of Stonehouse in 1989 and featured 55 high-backed seats. *Plaxton*

Plaxton's biggest UK rival in coach production, Duple, closed in 1989 and Plaxton took over the Duple service division and the production rights to the company's range of bus and coach bodies, with the exception of the Dartline body. Duple's 300 bus was abandoned, as was its high-floor 340 coach, but there were enough parts in stock to justify building a batch of 320 coach bodies. These were branded as the Plaxton 321, and 25 were built on Leyland Tiger chassis at Scarborough in 1990. Externally they were identical to the Duple product, but the interior was based on that used on Plaxton's Paramount models. Most 321s — 15 of them — went to Bebb of Llantwit Fardre.

Duple's 425 integral was an innovative coach with a rear-mounted Cummins L10 engine and a Cromweld body structure, and in 1990 Plaxton announced that the 425 would continue in production, but at Carosserie Lorraine. It was intended to offer 425s in 1991, but in the end it was 1992 before any were built. Plaxton relaunched the French-built 425 in February 1993 — then announced in March that it was closing Carosserie Lorraine. Only 12 examples of the 425 were built in France.

A lot was happening at Plaxton's Reeve Burgess subsidiary. In 1986 it launched what would turn out to be a long-lived best-seller — the Beaver. It started life as a small coach, with a single-piece inswing door, on the Mercedes-Benz 608D chassis. But it soon developed into a small bus, with two-piece door and prominent destination box, and as the 1980s progressed sales of Beaver buses took off.

Above: Plaxton's ownership of Carrosserie Lorraine saw a batch of 12 rear-engined Ivecos with Lorraine bodywork imported to the UK in 1990. One buyer was Skye-Ways of Kyle of Lochalsh, which used the compact coach on its service between Portree and Inverness. *Stewart J. Brown*

Right: One batch of Duple 320 bodies was built at Scarborough on Leyland Tiger chassis and promoted as the Plaxton 321, although it would take a sharp eye to spot the 321 badge on the grille. Externally the 321 was indistinguishable from the 320, but internally it was quite different, with an interior based on that of the Paramount. The 321 was sold through the Yeates dealership, owner of this demonstrator. *Stewart J. Brown*

PLAXTON : A Century of Innovation

Above: The Duple 425 was widely admired, and when Plaxton acquired the bulk of the Duple business it decided to produce the model in France, at the Carrosserie Lorraine plant. The vehicle was promoted as the Plaxton 425, but only 12 were built before decision was made to close the French factory. This is a demonstrator. *Plaxton*

Right: In the early days of production at Reeve Burgess the Beaver was built both as a coach and as a bus, all models featuring the shallow destination display seen on this Mercedes-Benz 709D running in Swansea with South Wales Transport. *Stewart J. Brown*

The Beaver was launched while Reeve Burgess was heavily involved in conversions of L608D vans to 20-seat buses; in 1986 alone it produced some 300 bus conversions for a range of NBC subsidiaries. Although most Beavers would be built on Mercedes chassis, the steel-framed body was also offered on the Iveco Daily and on the

Renault S56 and S75. Big Renault users included Mainline, in Sheffield, and the East London Bus & Coach Co. More than 1,000 Beavers had been built by 1991.

The Beaver was followed in 1988 by the Harrier on Leyland's new Swift chassis, which was powered by a mid-mounted Cummins B-series

engine. Although most were 37-seat coaches there were also a few Harrier buses and a few smaller coaches on short-wheelbase Swift chassis.

At the 1989 Coach & Bus show Reeve Burgess unveiled the 33-seat Beagle — which looked like a scaled-down Harrier — on the Iveco A70.14 chassis, with a front-mounted 5.9-litre 138bhp

engine. It was not a success, the only order coming from the London Borough of Croydon. The company also briefly diversified into ambulance production, setting up Reebur Ambulance in 1989.

In August 1990 Reeve Burgess released drawings of a new body, for the increasingly popular Dennis Dart midibus chassis. This was

Above: The Swift was Leyland's attempt to produce a low-cost midibus and was powered by a vertical mid-mounted Cummins B-series engine, which meant that it had a high floor. Probably the most attractive body offered on the Swift was the Reeve Burgess Harrier, available in two lengths and with up to 41 seats. Pennine of Gargrave took two 39-seaters in 1991. *Plaxton*

Left: The Harrier was an unusual type to find in operation with a major group. This Stagecoach vehicle was new to Hyndburn Transport and is seen in Accrington. *Stewart J. Brown*

Above: Iveco tried to secure a share of the small-bus market with a modified truck chassis, the A70.14, for which Reeve Burgess produced a slightly smaller version of the Harrier body, called the Beagle. The first vehicle to be completed was painted in a Plaxton corporate livery for the 1989 Coach & Bus show. The Iveco/Beagle combination was not a success. *Plaxton*

Right: The Beaver continued to sell well in the 1990s and was easily the most popular choice among operators looking for a small bus for use on lightly-used routes or over roads where bigger buses could not operate. This 27-seater was one of nine to enter service in South Wales with Rhondda in the winter of 1996/7. It was based on a Mercedes-Benz 711D. *Plaxton*

launched in January 1991 as the Pointer. The first went to Southampton Citybus. It differed from existing Reeve Burgess products in having an aluminium rather than a steel frame. And it was a runaway success. But it wasn't to be a success for Reeve Burgess. Plaxton decided to close the cramped and ageing Reeve Burgess factory in Pilsley, and this happened in July 1991. Production of the Pointer, Beaver and Harrier was transferred to Scarborough, while the Beagle was dropped. The Harrier had a short life at Scarborough, as Leyland discontinued the Swift chassis in 1991. In total around 125 Harriers were built, most of them at Pilsley. The Reeve Burgess name was briefly retained for the Pointer, but was quietly dropped during 1992.

The Coleman Milne and Mellor businesses were sold to their management in the spring of 1992, and at that time the rights to build the Beagle were acquired by Mellor.

The Paramount continued to sell well, and in spring 1991 the 5,000th was built, entering service with Paul S. Winson Coaches of Loughborough.

The Pointer small bus had a remarkable effect on Plaxton, at a time when coach sales were declining, and is widely acknowledged to have been the product which saved the Scarborough factory. The Pointer was purchased in large numbers by operators in London and was also popular elsewhere in the country, with both large and small operators. It was initially built in three lengths from 8.5 to 9.8m, seating from 35 to 43 people, with a choice of under-seat heaters or skirting radiators and the option of a split-step entrance to make access easier for passengers with impaired mobility.

Above: The Pointer was not only one of Plaxton's most successful products but also ranks among the most successful bus bodies ever built in the UK. The majority were built on Dennis Dart chassis. This Dart/Pointer is in operation with Docklands Transit in London. In the early days of Pointer production the vast majority were sold to London operators. *Plaxton*

Above: Dual-door Pointers were generally ordered by London fleets, but some went to Oxford, where Thames Transit used two-door vehicles. *Stewart J. Brown*

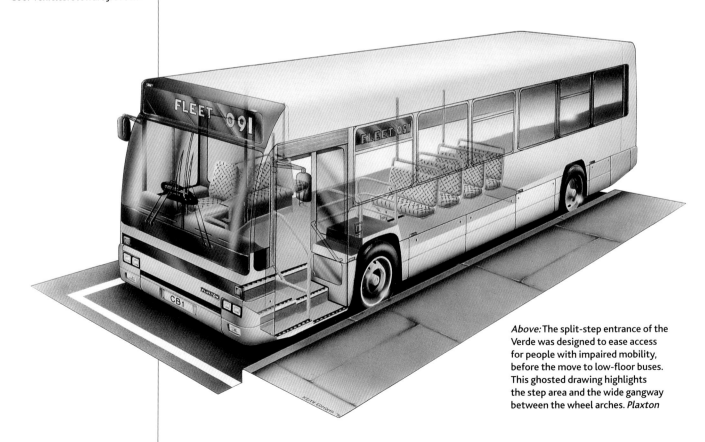

Above: The split-step entrance of the Verde was designed to ease access for people with impaired mobility, before the move to low-floor buses. This ghosted drawing highlights the step area and the wide gangway between the wheel arches. *Plaxton*

The success of the Pointer encouraged Plaxton to look at bigger buses, and in 1990 it announced the development of two new models — an 11.4m-long city bus and a double-decker.

The double-decker did not proceed much beyond some styling drawings, but the single-decker was unveiled in the spring of 1991 as the Verde, able to carry up to 52 seated passengers and with a total capacity of 75. This was an attractive design with a European look about it. The aluminium structure was developed from that used for the Pointer, although in terms of style the two bodies were quite different. It was the first bus to be designed to meet the requirements of DPTAC — the Disabled Persons Transport Advisory Committee. The Verde was launched on the Scania N113 chassis but was also offered on the Dennis Lance and, later, on the Volvo B10B. However, the first order was for none of these but came from Dublin Bus, which took 40 on DAF SB220 chassis.

A production batch of 15 Verdes was built on N113 chassis, 14 going to Cardiff City Transport in 1992 and the odd one becoming a Scania demonstrator, joining the original prototype; there was also a dual-door development vehicle, which

was later sold to Nottingham City Transport. These were the only Verdes built on Scania chassis, and it was on the Dennis Lance that the Verde would take off, thanks to major bus group Badgerline. In 1992 Badgerline ordered 77 Verdes on Dennis Lance chassis for 1993/4 delivery, and this was followed in 1994 by an order for 182 for 1995/6. The only trouble was that the Lance was a much lighter chassis than the N113, and after a period in service the Lance/Verde combination proved troublesome, requiring rectification work by both Plaxton and Dennis. In the end Badgerline took a total of 165 Verdes rather than the 259 it had ordered.

Between 1994 and 1997 the Verde was built on the Volvo B10B for a small number of operators including Cleveland Transit, Nottingham City Transport, Go-Ahead Gateshead and the Oxford Bus Company.

In all nearly 350 Verdes had been built by the time production ended in 1997, the majority of which were on Dennis Lance chassis. The biggest users were Yorkshire Rider and Midland Red West — both Badgerline-group companies — but Verdes were also bought by British Bus and by London Buses.

Above: The Verde was designed using the same principles as the Pointer, although the finished product looked quite different. It was built on chassis by DAF, Dennis, Scania and Volvo. Most were on Dennis Lance chassis, although the Lance/Verde combination proved not to be a happy one. The Verde was built between 1991 and 1997, its relatively short production life caused in part by the move to low-floor buses. This Lance was operated by Leeds City Link, part of the FirstBus business.
Stewart J. Brown

Above: Nottingham City Transport added five Verdes to its fleet in the spring of 1995. They were 51-seaters of Volvo B10B chassis; a sixth, with 47 seats, followed later in the year. They were part of a batch of nine built for stock, of which the other three were used as demonstrators by Plaxton and Volvo. *Stewart J. Brown*

Right: Dual-door Verdes were built for operation in London and Oxford. Those delivered to the Oxford Bus Company on Volvo B10B chassis in 1997 were the last Verdes to be built. *Stewart J. Brown*

Left: When the Verde was conceived there was the possibility that it could be developed as an articulated bus, as this artist's impression shows. Aware of plans for a guided busway in Leeds, the artist has included lateral guide wheels. *Plaxton*

Below: In the early 1990s consideration was being given to building a double-deck bus at Scarborough, and this artist's impression reveals Plaxton's thoughts on styling. Bearing in mind the conservatively styled vehicles being produced at that time by the main double-deck manufacturers — Alexander and Northern Counties — this was an attractive bus. This drawing shows a dual-door London-style vehicle with a split-step entrance. *Plaxton*

SIX

Buses Bring Growth

THE big news of 1991 was the launch of an all-new range of coaches. The Paramount had been available in three basic versions — 3200, 3500 and the double-deck 4000. The new models were offered in two heights, 3.2m and 3.5m, with a choice of frontal styling on the high-floor model. The standard coach was the Premiere 320 or 350. What Plaxton planned as a flagship was the 3.5m-high Excalibur, which featured a swept-back windscreen, a plug door and a revised interior treatment incorporating wrap-around front and rear ceiling panels, the front being designed to incorporate a video monitor. The Premiere had a more upright front, and an inswing door. The Excalibur also had a Continental door as standard; this was available as an option on the Premiere.

Having used gently curved side glass since 1968, Plaxton broke with that tradition on its new range, which featured tinted flat glass. The windows were shallower than on the Paramount, and the structure was the first to be available in Britain which met tough new European safety legislation. This was the R66 roll-over test, which was intended to ensure that if a coach rolled over the roof structure would not collapse, thus ensuring a

greater chance of survival for the occupants. Bonded double-glazing added to the structure's strength, and there were reinforcing pillars at the rear and ahead of the front axle, making the new Plaxtons among the world's safest coaches.

In place of traditional glass fibre mouldings the new range featured RTM — resin transfer moulding — which was more able to absorb minor impacts without breaking. This was used for the lower corner panels and the side locker doors. RTM had never been used before in coach manufacture, and it proved difficult to maintain consistent standards in production. It soon became apparent that it could not provide the standard of quality and consistency that Plaxton had hoped for, and a return to more conventional materials was made in 1992.

Plaxton spent £3.5 million in research and development on its new coaches, including wind-tunnel testing which showed that the new models were more aerodynamically efficient than the old range — something which, it was claimed, would improve fuel economy by 10%. The company had also invested £750,000 in computer-aided design and finite element analysis to enhance the design process. Finite element analysis allowed the

Right: A full-size mock-up was produced of the new coach range to be launched in 1991 as the Premiere and Excalibur. It captured the overall shape of the new model, although when the Excalibur appeared the windscreen would have slightly greater curvature, and the width of the pillar behind the door would be reduced slightly. *Stephen Barber collection*

company's design engineers to simulate different types of loads and stresses on the body structure, before carrying out punishing track tests at the Motor Industry Research Association's proving ground at Nuneaton.

Premiere and Excalibur were engineered initially for Volvo, Dennis and Scania chassis. Although a Scania-based Excalibur and a Premiere 320 were used to launch the range at Coach & Bus '91 in October, this turned out to be a short-lived combination, just one batch of Premiere 320s — including 30 for Shearings — and a handful of Premiere 350s being produced on Scania chassis.

At the launch more than 150 orders were placed for the new range, including 61 for Wallace Arnold, 40 for Shearings, 30 for Parks of Hamilton and 18 for Excelsior. A large number of smaller operators also placed orders. The vast majority of early Premieres and Excaliburs were built on Volvo B10M chassis. There was also an Expressliner version of the Premiere.

The Paramount 4000 remained available, but none was built after the new range appeared. To support fleet standardisation at Bus Éireann, Plaxton built a final batch of 20 Paramount 3500 bodies on DAF MB230 chassis in 1992.

In launching the new range Plaxton had, once again, an eye on sales in mainland Europe. When Volvo launched its new B12R in October 1991 one of the vehicles had a left-hand-drive version of the Excalibur body, called the Prestige 350. This was a two-door coach — with what counted as the Continental door on a UK-specification coach acting as a second entrance. There was also a 3.7m-high version, the Prestige 370.

In the summer of 1992 it was announced that Volvo and Plaxton were to work together, with Volvo selling Plaxton coaches in Europe and elsewhere. There was an optimistic forecast that this would involve 200 sales annually — but like many previous Plaxton attempts to sell in Europe this one soon foundered. Fewer than 20 B12Rs with Prestige bodies were produced, intended for the French market, although many were in fact sold to Italian operators.

When it was unveiled the new range was available only in 12m overall length, but in 1992 an 11m Premiere 320 was launched on the Dennis Javelin and a 10m version on the Volvo B10M. There were 10m Javelins too.

It was a measure of the success of the new range that it secured the biggest single coach order in Plaxton's history. This came from Stagecoach in 1992 and was for 150 Premieres — 100 Volvo B10Ms and 50 Dennis Javelins. These were to what was described as an interurban specification, which included destination indicators.

Above: The original Premiere 320 on a Volvo B10M chassis, posed in Hull shortly before the model's launch. The new range used shallower windows than previous models and marked a reversion to flat glass after 20 years of using curved side windows on most models. Tinted double-glazing was standard. *Plaxton*

Right: The Premiere 320 replaced the Paramount 3200 and was available on a range of chassis, including the Dennis Javelin. This example was operated by Woodward's of Glossop. *Plaxton*

Below: The Excalibur, with its deep, raked windscreen, was an eye-catching design. It was conceived as a flagship coach and was initially offered with a higher specification than the Premiere. Most Excaliburs were built on Volvo B10M chassis, like this coach operated by the Oxford Bus Company on its express services to London's two major airports. *Stewart J. Brown*

Above: The Premiere 350 was chosen as the basis for a new generation of National Expressliners. This one, on a Dennis Javelin GX, was operated by South Wales Transport on services between South Wales and London. *Dennis*

Right: The Prestige was developed as a 3.7m-high model on Volvo's rear-engined B12R chassis, with the intention of securing sales in France. The 3.7m-high model was not really suitable for a two-axle chassis, and most Prestiges were 3.5m high. Most went to Italian operators. *Plaxton*

Le nouveau

PRESTIGE

PLAXTON

Left: When the showroom was built at the Eastfield factory it was often used to hand over new coaches to customers large and small. One of the biggest was Wallace Arnold, and here, with a new Excalibur in the background, Plaxton Managing Director Neil Beresford makes a formal handover to Wallace Arnold Operations Director Stephen Barber. Looking on, from left to right, are Wallace Arnold Chief Engineer Eric Stockwell, Plaxton's Kevin Wood, Tony Harvey of dealer Yeates, Plaxton's Clive Hodgson, Glyn McKenzie of dealer Kirkby, Plaxton's Bob Walmsley and Wallace Arnold's David Braund. *Courtesy Bob Walmsley*

Where the Paramount range had evolved through various identifiable versions during its 10-year production life, there was no such face-lifting of the Premiere and Excalibur. The only major changes were in 1993, for the 1994 season, when the front was modified with the deletion of the air intakes below the number plate, and a revised rear end was introduced on which the rear window no longer curved into the roof line, a feature which had been a source of leaks. With the re-styled rear came new tail-light clusters.

In the summer of 1992 the Cowie group made a £28 million takeover bid for Henlys, the owners of Plaxton. Cowie ran car dealerships, operated buses in London and owned the Hughes DAF coach dealer in Cleckheaton. The bid was unsuccessful.

Meanwhile Plaxton's bus business was booming. The 500th Pointer was delivered in the summer of 1992 (to Cowie-owned London operator Grey-Green), and the 1,000th followed two years later, going to Badgerline subsidiary Thamesway.

Badgerline was an important Plaxton customer, and in 1994 placed not just the biggest order in Plaxton's history but one of the biggest single orders ever placed with a British bus body-builder. This was for 843 vehicles, made up of 339 Pointers, 317 Beavers and the aforementioned 182 Verdes.

Most Pointer bodies were built on Dennis Dart chassis, but when Volvo entered the midibus market in 1992, with the B6R, the Pointer was re-engineered to fit the Volvo chassis. The first B6R/Pointer went to Mainline in Sheffield, and

Right: Pointer bodies on the Volvo B6 could be identified by a step in the window line at the rear emergency door — effectively disguised on this Mainline bus by the application of black paint which gives the appearance of a continuous straight waist. There is a small Volvo badge to the left of the registration number. *Stewart J. Brown*

later significant orders (on what was by then known as the Volvo B6) came from Merseybus, which took 50, and from Mainline, Maidstone & District and OK Motor Services. In total Plaxton bodied just over 150 B6s, most of them in 1994.

In April 1994, to cope with increased demand for Pointers, Plaxton moved production of the Beaver to a new facility alongside the company's service centre at Anston. This became known as the small bus division.

There was growing demand in the 1990s for improved access to urban buses for people with impaired mobility, and both Dennis and Volvo revised their midibus models to create the Dart SLF (Super Low Floor) and B6LE (Low Entry). These were launched at Coach & Bus '95 with improved Pointer bodies. The basic styling was similar, but the structure was new, with a strong cantrail to compensate for the reduced rigidity of the new generation of low-floor chassis. Where in the past the chassis had in general supported the body, now there was a change of emphasis. Both chassis- and body-builders had to work together much more closely, and the body-builder had greater responsibility to ensure the strength of the completed vehicle.

The new low-floor Pointer was wider — 2.4m instead of 2.3m. This answered the main passenger criticism of the original model — restricted space — and also created more room for wheelchair users to manœuvre and for parents with baby buggies. However, to achieve the same seating capacity as the original step-entrance models required an increase in length of around 600mm. The old models ranged in length from 8.5 to 9.9m (on the Volvo B6), whereas the new low-floor versions were between 9.2 and 10.6m long, while still seating between 35 and 43.

Only one B6LE was fitted with a Plaxton body for the UK; a further 20 were built for export to Hong Kong. From here on the Pointer was available exclusively on the Dennis Dart. The first low-floor Pointer entered service with Thamesway in March 1996.

Production of the original step-entrance Pointer continued throughout 1996 and then slowed dramatically in 1997 as more and more operators switched to the low-floor model. The last of the old-style Pointers for operation on the British mainland went to Stagecoach East London towards the end of 1997. One final batch of five was built in the spring of 1998 for operation in Jersey, where the narrower 2.3m width was needed. Around 2,000 step-entrance Pointers were produced.

Among the more unusual Pointers built in 1996 were 10 for Southampton Citybus which featured roof-mounted tanks to store compressed natural gas. A similar CNG-fuelled Pointer Dart was built for FirstBus and was trialled in Bristol.

The Pointer was given an Ogle make-over in 1997, with more attractive frontal styling, and in this guise became the Pointer 2.

Above: When Dennis introduced the Dart SLF — Super Low Floor — Plaxton produced a modified Pointer body to go with it. The structure was different, with more strength in the cantrail, and the body was 100mm wider, at 2.4m, addressing a criticism of the original Pointer over its limited interior width. First Glasgow received this low-floor Pointer in 1997. *Stewart J. Brown*

Above: The 1990s saw a small number of experiments with alternative fuels, and Plaxton built Pointers with roof-mounted fuel tanks on Dennis Dart chassis which were powered by CNG — compressed natural gas. First operated this vehicle in Bristol. CNG-fuelled Pointer Darts also operated in Southampton and Southport. *Stewart J. Brown*

Below: In 1997 the low-floor Pointer had a facelift, the styling work being carried out by Ogle. The structure and the windscreens were unchanged, but a new front panel and new lighting units softened the appearance of the body. Worth's of Enstone operated this Pointer 2. *Plaxton*

Left: Early Pointer 2s for FirstBus were built before the adoption of a corporate livery, as seen on this bus in Bolton, in a short-lived cream and blue colour scheme used for Gold Service buses. No fewer than 55 Pointer 2s on 10.7m Dart chassis were delivered to First's Greater Manchester fleet in 1997. *Stewart J. Brown*

Below: The Pointer 2 sold well to small bus operators around the country. These included Mitcham Belle, which for a short period operated contracted services in South London. Its first buses were 12 Dennis Darts with Pointer 2 bodywork, delivered in 1999. *Plaxton*

Right: Plaxton has been a regular supplier over the years to local operator Scarborough & District, a subsidiary of East Yorkshire. The company operated a large fleet of Beavers in the town and in 1999 introduced five Pointer 2s on 10.7m Dennis Dart chassis. These were followed in 2000 by 13 Mini Pointer Darts. *Stewart J. Brown*

The Beaver continued to be Britain's most popular small bus, and in 1996 Plaxton announced the Beaver 2, production of which started in 1997. The Beaver 2 was developed for the new Mercedes-Benz Vario chassis, which featured air suspension. The chassis layout allowed a lower floor with a height of 650mm against 720mm on the original Beaver, and an entrance layout which met DPTAC requirements.

Ogle styled the new Beaver, although under the skin the structure was largely as before. Three models were available, in lengths of 7m (with

Right: The Beaver 2 had a new roofline and a more prominent destination display as part of the standard specification. It was offered only on the Mercedes-Benz Vario chassis. Most of the big groups operated Beavers, including First, which had them in a number of subsidiaries from Aberdeen to Cornwall. This one went to PMT. *Plaxton*

23 seats), 7.8m (27 seats) and 8.5m (31 seats). Indicative of the popularity of Plaxton's small bus, initial orders for Beaver 2 included 207 for FirstBus and 100 for Stagecoach. While the Beaver was essentially a UK model, one batch was exported, to Transmac of Macau.

There were developments in the coach range in 1995. First, availability of the Premiere was extended to include the DAF SB3000 underframe. Premiere bodywork had previously been available only on the Volvo B10M and Dennis Javelin, with just the odd DAF against a specific order. The first DAF/Premieres for the UK were delivered in the spring of 1996 to Godsons of Leeds and Bibbys of Ingleton.

The Excalibur was also made available on the Javelin GX — a higher-powered version of the Javelin chassis — and the first, surprisingly, went to a country where there were second-hand Plaxton coaches but no new ones: Malta.

The last single-deck, three-axle coach to have been bodied by Plaxton for a UK operator was a twin-steer Panorama Elite-bodied Bedford VAL in 1972. That changed in 1995 with the appearance of an Excalibur body on a Volvo B12T for Dodsworth of Boroughbridge. The benefit of three axles was that it guaranteed high-specification coaches could operate comfortably within legal weight limits — something which on some two-axle chassis/body combinations could be problematic if the vehicle was fully laden.

The Dodsworth Excalibur B12T was exhibited at Coach & Bus '95. It was never intended to be a high-volume model, and just under two dozen

were sold. The biggest users were First, which had seven for the Reading–Heathrow express service, and Nottingham City Coaches, which had four.

But the big coaching development of 1995, in more ways than one, was an order from Stagecoach for 10 Premiere articulated coaches. These were based on Volvo B10MA chassis and were the first — and, so far, only — articulated coaches to be built in Britain. They were 18m long and seated 71 — 20 more than a standard 12m-long Stagecoach Plaxton Premiere Interurban. They were initially operated by Fife, Ribble and East Midland.

Above: Export Beavers were rare. This is part of a batch delivered to Transmac in Macau, which were of dual-door layout and air-conditioned. *Plaxton*

Left: The Premiere was also available on DAF chassis. Seen at the Brighton coach rally in 1996 with Bibby's of Ingleton is a rear-engined SB3000, one of a batch of 10 built for the Hughes DAF dealership. *Stewart J. Brown*

There were big moves afoot in 1995. Henlys and Volvo jointly purchased Prevost, a Canadian coach and motorhome manufacturer with an enviable reputation for high-quality vehicles. When the deal was concluded there was talk of exporting Plaxton-bodied Volvo B12Ts to North America, but like many previous export plans this came to nought.

At the same time as Henlys was establishing a presence in North America it made a rather more modest but still significant acquisition: Northern Counties of Wigan. Northern Counties was an old-established bus builder which had been through troubled times. It went into administration in 1991 and was then rescued by a management buy-out in 1992. The acquisition gave Henlys a double-deck bus, the Palatine, and two versions of the Paladin single-decker; these were a midi, on the Dart and B6, and a full-size model, offered on various chassis. The midibus competed head-on with the Pointer. The full-size Paladin was a Verde competitor. Both models were phased out in 1996 — not simply because they duplicated existing Plaxton models but also because operators were moving to low-floor buses.

When Henlys acquired the business Northern Counties was developing an attractive new low-floor single-deck body, the first being built on a DAF SB220 chassis. This was launched as the Paladin LF at Coach & Bus '95. It would be early 1997 before the first production vehicles appeared, these being five for Stagecoach Manchester on Volvo B10BLE chassis. During 1997 production was transferred from Wigan to Scarborough, and the body renamed from Northern Counties Paladin LF to the snappier Plaxton Prestige, conveniently forgetting the use of that name for export B12R coaches as recently as 1994. The vast majority of Prestige bodies — almost 150 — were on DAF chassis. Arriva was the biggest user, with 54 DAFs running for its subsidiaries in the North East of England, and smaller numbers elsewhere, including nine with coach seats for operation on a Green Line service. Other unusual Prestiges were 19 dual-door 30-seaters for Speedlink, to operate a temporary shuttle service between Heathrow Airport and Heathrow Junction pending completion of the Heathrow Express rail link from Paddington station to the airport. A small number of the DAFs ran on LPG and had gas-storage tanks on their roofs. Prestige production ended in 1999, the last vehicles being for Arriva The Shires.

That Prestige production totalled fewer than 150 vehicles is a measure of the trend away from heavy-duty single-deckers towards lighter

Above: The first articulated coaches to be built in Britain were Plaxton Premiere 320s, on Volvo B10M chassis for Stagecoach, in 1995. Ten were produced, for use on busy express services. This coach started life with Ribble but was later moved north to join the Fife fleet, for use on services to Glasgow. *Stewart J. Brown*

Left: The Prestige name was reused for a low-floor single-deck model which had been developed by Northern Counties as the Paladin LF. The biggest concentration of Plaxton Prestige buses was in the North East of England, where they were operated by Arriva and Go Northern, one of whose DAF SB220s is seen entering Gateshead, pursued by an Arriva Pointer Dart. *Stewart J. Brown*

Right: The extra-long Super Pointer Dart was favoured by a number of municipally-owned fleets including Cardiff, Plymouth and, as seen here, Thamesdown. From 1992 to 2004 the Dart/Pointer, in a variety of specifications, was Thamesdown's standard bus. *Stewart J. Brown*

models, as epitomised by the Pointer Dart, in a growing number of variations. One that challenged models such as the Prestige was launched at Coach & Bus '97 — the Super Pointer Dart. This had been developed as a result of close co-operation between engineers at Plaxton and Dennis and stretched the Dart concept to the maximum length it could reach while retaining the existing wheels and axles. This produced a bus which was 11.3m long, typically with up to 41 seats — which compared with only four more seats in the heavier and more expensive Prestige. The Super Pointer Dart thus offered high carrying capacity in a medium-weight package. It secured orders from, among others, Arriva, FirstGroup, Go-Ahead, Stagecoach, Thamesdown Transport and Plymouth Citybus — although some fleet engineers were wary of the concept of a big bus based on a vehicle that had started out as a midi.

The other major — and most successful — adaptation of the Pointer followed in 1998 as the Mini Pointer Dart. This shrunk the vehicle to create an 8.8m 26-seater, designed to replace older high-floor minibuses — such as early Beavers. It was an instant success. It used proven components with a high degree of parts commonality with bigger Pointer models, and it offered step-

Right: The Mini Pointer Dart, just 8.8m long, was developed jointly by Plaxton and Dennis as a replacement for step-entrance minibuses.
It was more expensive than a Beaver 2 but offered access for wheelchairs and had a heavier-duty chassis.
Scarlet Band of West Cornforth was one of many small operators to buy this compact model. *Plaxton*

free access on routes where big buses could not be used. It also benefited from disenchantment with early Mercedes Varios, which had proved troublesome in operation and had encouraged operators to consider alternatives. Very soon the Mini Pointer Dart would be in service with operators large and small throughout Britain, being bought by most of the big groups and by a large number of small businesses.

The Pointer was also securing sales overseas — notably in Canada, Hong Kong and Iceland.

There were moves afoot in small coaches too. Although conceived as a coach, the Beaver had quickly been accepted as a bus. Small numbers were still being fitted out as coaches, but the Beaver wasn't what coach operators wanted. So, using the same Mercedes-Benz Vario chassis, Plaxton designed a purpose-built coach, the Cheetah. This retained the Mercedes grille but with a new bonnet and raked-back windscreen. The floor level was raised, to give a flat floor with no wheelarch intrusion. The Cheetah had bonded glazing and a single-piece inswing door. Typically built as a 33-seater, it was soon being specified with various other layouts, including a 29-seater, with room for a larger boot, and an executive coach, with 16 leather seats, air-conditioning, servery and washroom.

Above: Plaxton secured a number of export orders for the Pointer, from such diverse locations as Iceland, Hong Kong and Canada. Two Canadian vehicles are seen here with Whistler Transit. They are air-conditioned and have fixed double-glazed windows. Other alterations for Canada included extra marker lights on the front dome and on the body side. *Dennis*

Left: The Cheetah, built exclusively on the Mercedes-Benz Vario chassis, brought new style to small coaches and quickly established itself as the leader in the small-coach market. Customers have included Johnsons of Henley-in-Arden. *Plaxton*

Above: Many operators buy both large and small coaches from Plaxton. In 1999 Biss Coaches of Bishops Stortford took a Cheetah and an Excalibur. The Cheetah was on a Mercedes-Benz Vario chassis, the Excalibur on a Volvo B10M. *Plaxton*

The Cheetah set new standards in small coaches, and, despite increasing competition since its launch in 1997, annual sales have grown from around 60 in 1998 to more than 100 in 2004 and 2005, making it Britain's best-selling small coach. Initially it was built alongside full-size coaches in Scarborough, but in 1998 production was transferred to the Small Bus Division at Anston. Although small batches are sometimes produced at Scarborough, to balance capacity with demand, Cheetah production remains at Anston, where it is built alongside the Beaver.

Back in 1990 Plaxton had toyed with the idea of building a double-deck bus. The takeover of Northern Counties in 1995 gave the Henlys group instant access to the double-deck market with the established and successful Palatine I and Palatine II models. These were built mainly on Volvo Olympian chassis, but there were small numbers on Scania N113, Dennis Arrow and DAF DB250 chassis.

Under Henlys control the company developed a new low-floor double-deck model, unveiled to widespread acclaim at Coach & Bus '97 as the Plaxton President.

It was built to the newly legal width of 2.55m rather than the old 2.5m maximum, and the show exhibit was on a Volvo B7L chassis — a model that Volvo had yet to launch in the UK.

Volvo was reluctant to say much about the chassis, and perhaps wisely so, for its layout, with a long rear overhang and the engine in the rear offside corner, drew sharp criticism. But none of

that detracted from the praise for the body. It had deep windscreens, bonded side glass, and a stylish interior in which, for the first time on a British bus, the vertical handrails were curved outwards towards the top to create an impression of space and modernity.

The 10.5m-long two-door bus was painted red, and it was said at the launch that it would enter service in London in 1998. It didn't. Indeed, it never entered service at all. Plaxton had worked with Volvo in good faith, but the B7L was the wrong chassis for a UK double-decker, as Volvo soon admitted. So development work on the President was then concentrated on two other chassis — the Dennis Trident and the low-floor version of the DAF DB250 — until Volvo came up with the improved B7TL model with a transverse rear engine.

The President was the star of the 1997 show, and it was soon winning orders. Early buyers on Trident chassis included Metroline with 65 and First with 130. Travel West Midlands ordered 102 on the Volvo B7TL, while Arriva London ordered 20 on DAF chassis.

The first Presidents entered service in London with Metroline in March 1999. A few months later the last of the old-style Palatines entered service in London with First subsidiary CentreWest, and with them came the end of the Northern Counties name.

Plaxton offered various options on the President including a centre exit — specified by London operators and by Lothian Buses — and either

bonded or gasket glazing. As a general rule London buses had gasket glazing, although early deliveries to the capital featured bonded windows.

Coaches, meanwhile, were getting more complex, more luxurious and more expensive. By the mid-1990s virtually all new Plaxton coaches had reclining seats, the majority had toilets, and a growing number had air-conditioning.

Recognising the need for a simpler, less expensive, model, Volvo introduced the B7R to the UK market in 1997 and teamed up with Plaxton which provided a version of the Premiere 320 with a simpler specification, known as the Prima. The basic concept for the body had been seen a year earlier on a batch of 15 Dennis Javelin chassis sold through Kirkby as the Premiere Express, which incorporated a simpler interior to distinguish it from the Premiere 320. For the Prima the specification was further revised, making use of new interior trims to give it a more attractive appearance but still aimed at budget-conscious buyers. The result was far from spartan and was to carve a new niche in the market. The Prima B7R was launched at Coach & Bus '97 and after a slow start soon proved to be a popular choice for operators wanting a good-quality coach for local hires and excursions. The Prima, which was externally indistinguishable from a Premiere, was later made available on the Dennis Javelin and DAF SB3000 chassis.

One aspect of Plaxton's output which has remained consistent but largely unnoticed for more than 30 years is the production of high-capacity single-deck coaches typically used for bus services and school transport; by virtue of using 3+2 seating and an offset gangway, seating capacity could be increased by up to 20%. This had started as early as 1972 with a batch of Elite II Express coaches for Barton Transport which seated 64, although the concept dated back to the 1960s, when examples of the Derwent bus were built to this configuration. The Barton vehicles were the first coach bodies to adopt this layout. Within a few years 12m Elites for Weardale Motor Services pushed seating capacity to 68. In 1998 a 70-seat Prima was added to the range to cater for this market. High-backed coach seats, complete with three-point seatbelts, and plenty of locker space made this an attractive option for operators in both the private and public sectors.

Above: The Plaxton President was built in Wigan at the former Northern Counties plant, which had been extensively modernised to produce the new low-floor model. It was available in a range of specifications on DAF, Dennis and Volvo chassis. This early-production President, on a Dennis Trident chassis for London operator Metroline, features bonded glazing, which was relatively unusual on a London bus. *Dennis*

Henlys was still on the expansion trail. At the end of 1997 Prevost — owned jointly by Henlys and Volvo — purchased NovaBus, a builder of urban buses for the North American market. And in 1999 Henlys, acting on its own, bought US schoolbus builder Blue Bird. Blue Bird was building around 14,000 vehicles a year. With the first signs of interest among British authorities in running purpose-built school buses, Leicester-based Alan Wilson had been appointed a Blue Bird dealer in 1994, and this saw small numbers being imported for Staffordshire and Sussex county councils. Plaxton explored the sales potential for Blue Birds which it would import from the USA, with the intention that, initially at least, Alan Wilson would remain as a dealer.

In the summer of 1998 came yet another turning point for Plaxton. At this stage the company was primarily a bus builder, and its key product was the Pointer. Consequently its key chassis supplier was Dennis — mainly with Darts but also with some Javelin coach chassis. There was increasing co-operation between the two companies, and in July a merger was announced which would unite the two businesses to create a £640 million bus and coach manufacturing group. The news was well received, but then the Mayflower group — owner of the Alexander bus-building business in Falkirk — decided it wanted

control of Dennis and that it could offer Dennis shareholders a better deal than the proposed Henlys merger.

Volvo, which was collaborating with Henlys in North America, then took a 10% stake in the Henlys business and voiced its support for the original merger proposals. But to Dennis shareholders short-term gain was more important than long-term strategy, and in October the Plaxton/Dennis merger proposal collapsed, and Mayflower took control of Dennis.

This meant that ownership of Plaxton's main chassis supplier was now in the hands of the group which owned a rival body-builder, raising fears that Mayflower would seek to promote Alexander bodywork on Dennis chassis at Plaxton's expense. Plaxton was soon working on a new project — Bus 2000 — which it was developing as an integral bus to succeed the Dart/Pointer combination and protect its position as a major bus manufacturer.

Alongside Bus 2000 there was a Coach 2000 project, developing the next generation of Plaxton coaches, to succeed the existing Excalibur, Premiere and Prima ranges. The new coach models were unveiled at Coach & Bus '99 as the Panther and Paragon. Like Excalibur and Premiere 350 they were identical structures with different styles of front end. Panther was the

flagship model, with a raked windscreen and plug door; Paragon was the standard model. Both were 3.5m high and were also 2.55m wide. A key improvement over the previous range was the use of a Cromweld steel structure, to resist corrosion, and multiplex wiring which was simpler to install and made fault-finding easier. There were teething problems with the multiplex system, and for a time some coaches were produced with conventional wiring where operators requested it.

Externally, Plaxton returned to deeper side windows using curved glass, with a gentle downward sweep of the waistline above the front axle. Inside, the extra 50mm made the coach seem much roomier than such a small increase in width would suggest, and the floor was gently ramped at the front to create a tiered effect for the first three rows of seats. Plaxton's designers had optimised use of the interior space, giving better legroom on a standard 53-seater than was possible on most competing coaches. The use of computer-aided design and finite element analysis in developing the structure also ensured that, at a time when coaches were getting heavier, the new models were lighter than most other 12m designs.

There were prestigious orders for the new range, from companies including Wallace Arnold, Shearings, National Holidays and Parks of Hamilton. The first to go into service were striking black-liveried Paragons for Parks.

The new coaches were initially available only on the Volvo B10M chassis, and in 2000 Plaxton was building both its new and its old ranges. Indeed, one of the year's biggest orders, from Bus Éireann, was for 58 B10M/Excaliburs and 55 B7R/Primas.

There was no 3.2m-high version of Coach 2000, so when the Excalibur and Premiere were finally discontinued the Prima remained available. In 2003 this was extensively updated, with a Paragon-style front panel and a revised rear, as well as a new interior, and renamed the Profile. This was a successful update and ensured a continued life for the body, still on B7R and Javelin chassis. A 10m Profile on Dennis Javelin chassis was added to the range in 2006.

Availability of the Paragon and Panther was extended to the new Dennis R-series in 2000, the new Volvo B12M and B12B in 2000 and 2002 respectively, the Iveco EuroRider in 2001 and, most recently, to the MAN 18.310 and 18.360 in 2006.

Above: The original Prima was this vehicle based on a Volvo B7R and exhibited by Plaxton at Coach & Bus '97. The Prima was later made available on Dennis Javelin and DAF SB3000. *Plaxton*

Right: The Bus 2000 project was conceived as an alternative to the Dennis Dart, but was dropped when Henlys merged with Mayflower to form TransBus. This prototype was purchased by Northumbria Coaches. *Gary Mitchellhill*

Below: The Panther was the first Plaxton coach to be built to the new legal maximum width of 2.55m. It had deeper windows than the previous range and slight curvature to the waist at the front, which echoed the use of a sloping front section on the saloon floor. This example, on Volvo B10M chassis, went to Paul James of Coalville. *Plaxton*

Above: Just as there had been alternative front-end profiles on the Excalibur and Premiere, there were two frontal styles on the new range, the Paragon having a more upright front — although the difference was not always immediately apparent when viewed from the front. Don Prentice of Haddington was the owner of this Paragon on a Dennis R-series underframe. *Plaxton*

Left: Cambridgeshire-based Kenzies Coaches is a long-established user of Plaxton products. In 2005 the company added to its fleet this Panther, for use on holidays for leading tour operator Globus. It was based on a Volvo B12B. *Plaxton*

Right: Demonstrating the 70 seat capacity of the Profile, a group of schoolchildren board a Volvo B7R delivered to Leicestershire County Council in 2005 for operation on school contracts. The Profile offers a higher standard of comfort for field trips by schools than is available on most purpose-designed lower-cost yellow school buses. *Plaxton*

Below: New in 2006 was a 10m version of the Profile on Dennis Javelin chassis. Pulham's Coaches of Bourton-on-the-Water, which operates a mainly Plaxton fleet, took this 41-seater. *Plaxton*

Left: In 2005 wheelchair-accessible 12.8m-long Paragons were specified by a small number of operators, including Gordons of Rotherham, which took this Volvo B12M. Wheelchair access was by means of a lift located just ahead of the rear wheels. The dark-tinted bonded glazing hides the additional 800mm-long window which is located above the Gordons fleetname. *Plaxton*

Left: From 2006 the Panther body was made available on MAN 18.310 and 18.360 chassis. The first, for Gloucestershire operator Applegates, is seen here ready for delivery from MAN dealer Mentor Coach & Bus. *Mentor*

Left: Only the badging reveals that underneath this Paragon is an Iveco EuroRider chassis, an option available to Plaxton customers since 2001. The Irisbus logo appears above the numberplate, the EuroRider badge alongside the entrance. The operator was Chambers of Stevenage. *Plaxton*

SEVEN

Building for a Strong Future

THE 1990s had drawn to a close with a degree of bitterness harboured in both the Henlys and Mayflower camps, created in the heat of the takeover battle for Dennis. Mayflower had won that round, but what lay ahead in the next decade would soon reduce the importance of that particular battle.

The takeover of Dennis by Mayflower had left Plaxton looking vulnerable, and on 1 August 2000 there came an announcement which some saw as inevitable. Henlys and Mayflower were to merge their UK bus-manufacturing interests in a new company, TransBus International. Mayflower would contribute the Alexander, Metsec and Dennis operations, together with their respective aftermarket services, to take a 70% stake. Henlys would contribute its UK-based manufacturing and distribution operations, essentially Plaxton, Northern Counties — by that stage known as Plaxton Wigan — and Kirkby in return for a 30% stake.

Although there was significant overcapacity in the UK body-building industry TransBus denied that it would close any of its manufacturing facilities. It did, however, institute a benchmarking exercise among its plants to assess where improvements to productivity could be made. In addition to Plaxton's three sites — at Scarborough, Anston and Wigan — TransBus had two Alexander factories to keep busy, at Falkirk and Belfast. There was also a need for product rationalisation.

Alexander's ALX100 minibus on the Vario was no match for Plaxton's Beaver in terms of sales success. The Beaver survived; the ALX100 did not. The ALX200 on the Dart SLF had sold well but was still outclassed by the Pointer, and ALX200 production ceased at the end of 2001. On double-deckers both the ALX400 and the President had enough customers to justify retention, although not enough volume to justify building double-deckers at three different locations. But both continued in production until 2005. The Bus 2000 project was largely abandoned, although its front-end styling would be used by TransBus for its new Enviro300 single-decker, and development of the frame structure was completed to form the basis of a number of Blue Bird vehicles for the North American market.

One all-new Plaxton project was developed under TransBus ownership: a minibus body on the Mercedes-Benz Sprinter. This project was conceived early in 2002, but initial uncertainty on the part of TransBus about a market in which it had little experience saw the project put to one side in favour of more pressing commitments. By the spring of 2003 it was back on the agenda, and development was underway. Announced in November 2003, the Pronto was aimed primarily at the public- and private-sector markets for demand-responsive transport; it had a welded Cromweld steel frame, using technology similar to that of the Panther and Paragon, direct glazing and a flat floor in the main saloon area, with no wheelarch intrusion. Tracking on the floor provided secure anchorage points for wheelchair users, who boarded using a lift at the rear of the vehicle. It could seat up to 16 people.

The decision by TransBus to drop the ALX200 bus body proved not to be good news for Plaxton: TransBus decided that it would now produce the Pointer range at Falkirk rather than Scarborough and in the spring of 2001 announced that the Scarborough facility was to close, with the loss of 750 jobs. It was the only TransBus factory building steel-framed bodies, and transferring coach production to one of the group's other sites would have been difficult. Thus coach production would either cease entirely or be transferred to some other location, Hungary — where TransBus had inherited a development facility previously owned by Plaxton — being rumoured as the favourite.

Overall, the coach division was performing badly. There was too much stock — some 300 used vehicles at Kirkby and 60 new coaches at Plaxton — and in some reckoning the business was actually losing £5,000 on each coach it built. Competition was an issue too, with eight significant dealers looking for business in a shrinking market. Plaxton also faced 15 European

competitors, and the low value of the Euro added to the company's troubles, making imported vehicles unrealistically price-competitive. It also virtually wiped out Plaxton's previously buoyant exports to Ireland.

The tourist market in the UK was suffering badly as a result of the foot-and-mouth outbreak in the winter of 2000/1. This affected tour bookings, and coach operators were finding their workloads reduced. For perhaps the first time in its history Plaxton had to bear the burden of a significant number of cancelled orders, and finding homes for these coaches in a market already under strain would be a major challenge and had a major influence on the decisions taken.

A young Scot, Brian Davidson, had arrived at Scarborough in the midst of the closure announcement and, after making an assessment of the situation, saw some benefit in retaining the plant for steel-framed coach production as opposed to what might prove to be a lengthy interruption in the supply of Plaxton products were it to move elsewhere. There were urgent negotiations with the workforce at Scarborough, and to save the plant a scheme was drawn up which saw new working agreements with a slimmed-down workforce, reduced from 750 to just 226. The basic wage was reduced, but productivity bonuses were re-established; these had previously been consolidated in the basic rate. Agreement was reached on annualised hours to accommodate the seasonal nature of coach

production. A new culture was established, aimed at eliminating old adversarial ways. The last Plaxton-built Pointer — destined for Iceland — left the factory in July 2001, whereupon Scarborough reverted to its traditional role as a builder of coaches, the site now occupying 200,000sq ft rather than 600,000.

TransBus invested £1.2 million in reorganising production, and the factory ceased production for three months. There were no compulsory redundancies among workers on the shop floor, and before people were given the option of taking redundancy there were presentations to explain how the new business would work, so that people who felt they wanted to stay could make an informed choice.

Although the slimmed-down business was making the same vehicles on the same site, there were major changes. All production processes were examined, and the factory laid out for maximum efficiency, with all manufacturing in one factory — there would be no movement of part-built vehicles outside the main building. Lean manufacturing techniques were introduced, to cut down on costly inventory. The workforce played a major role in remodelling the plant. A small team of consultants was employed to maximise the benefits available, but as the entire 'new' workforce had been employed in the plant previously, they saw at first hand how things had gone wrong before, so were ideally placed to put them right.

Rationalisation on the site reduced the manufacturing area to little more than a third of that previously occupied. One casualty was the showroom, which sat at the main entrance and provided a prominent portal through which customers entered the plant. With such radical change and the whole plant itself now providing a prominent showcase for the business, the loss of just one icon which had in any case become synonymous with the Henlys era, was considered a small price to pay.

Initially the inherited brands had been retained, prefixed with 'TransBus' and adopting a new corporate style to encompass the group identity. The Plaxton business thus became known as TransBus Plaxton, but as the group developed its strategy based firmly on the TransBus brand, so the Plaxton suffix, together with Dennis, Alexander and Kirkby, were all quietly dropped in 2002, and the company became TransBus International Coach.

Coaches started to appear as TransBus products. The arctic tern disappeared, and all communications omitted any reference to Plaxton, but for the sharp-eyed the Plaxton name could still be spotted on the back of the company's coaches, where it was incorporated in the polished moulding above the number plate. And the Plaxton name was preserved in another context. When redundant areas of the site were sold to become a business park, with them came a new address for the TransBus International Coach business — Plaxton Park.

His job in restoring the business to a viable entity complete, Brian Davidson left in March 2003 to specialise in advising companies in a similar position to that which Plaxton had found itself in 2001. His replacement was Mike Keaney, a sharp Mancunian with a lifetime of experience in commercial vehicle manufacturing. Keaney brought an outside and impartial view of the operation and was able to see it in a different light from those who had previously been an integral part of it. His contribution was less revolution, more evolution, initiating further refinements to turn an already good plant into an outstanding one.

Under the guidance of Sales Director Kevin Wood, who had risen through the ranks in the Plaxton sales team since joining the company in 1976, sales success in the TransBus period saw production of full-size coaches rise to 247 in 2003 — up more than 10% in just two years. In the same year more than 200 small vehicles emerged from the Anston Small Bus facility.

The majority of these coaches were sold through the Anston coach-sales operation, which had improved performance dramatically, stock levels being reduced from over 300 at the end of 2000 to under 100 just three years later. The General Manager of the Anston sales operation, Glynn McKenzie, retired in 2003, Sales Manager Mick McElhone assuming responsibility for Anston sales from that time.

Throughout 2003 there was speculation that the Mayflower Group's debts were spiralling to a point which could destabilise the group. By the start of 2004 the situation had become public knowledge, and the group acknowledged some difficulty, although the true scale of the problem was yet to emerge. In February 2004 Mayflower issued its second profit warning in just a few months, and the group's financial position came under increasing scrutiny.

In early April 2004 Mayflower finally collapsed, the culmination of several days seemingly perched on the edge of a financial abyss. TransBus quickly followed, administrators for both companies being appointed on the same day.

Financial Controller of the former Plaxton operation was Julie Globe. Having transferred from the Anston arm of the business in August 2001, she had faced the difficulties in keeping the cash flowing to pay creditors and maintain the supply of materials which were the life-blood of the business whilst still having to service payments to Mayflower which were keeping the banks at bay and maintaining the ailing group afloat.

Now the situation was almost surreal. The supplier base had been cut, and any ability to pay the bills and keep suppliers on-board was now in the hands of an outside party whose sole intention was to realise as much value as possible from the assets. The situation developed quickly on the first full day of administration as the familiar face of Brian Davidson returned, by this time back within TransBus as Director of Aftermarket Services. Together with Mike Keaney, Kevin Wood and Julie Globe, Davidson, backed by venture capitalists Aberdeen Murray Johnstone and Barclays Bank, mounted a buy-out bid which would rescue the former Plaxton business.

The bid was considered by the administrators, but initial hopes that it would be the only one soon faded as other parties registered an interest in the business. The fortunes during this period of grave uncertainty ebbed and flowed as, one by one, prospective buyers took stock, and the outlook for the continuation of manufacturing in Scarborough and Anston looked increasingly bleak. It seemed as though overseas buyers, intent on asset stripping, were willing to pay a premium price for the technology and resources of the company. At the eleventh hour, however, the management team was invited back to the table, and a deal was swiftly concluded which saw the former Plaxton business return to private ownership.

It emerged that Brian Davidson, even before the TransBus collapse, had been planning to make an offer for the business. This enabled him to move quickly with the company's management to make

Above: The entire new team at Plaxton ranged alongside a Paragon — for Logans Executive Travel of Ballymena — when the successful buy-out was announced. In the foreground are (from left to right) Kevin Wood, Brian Davidson, Mike Keaney and Julie Globe. *Scarborough Evening News*

an offer. Initially the administrators, determined to sell TransBus as a whole, had rejected the idea of selling Plaxton in isolation, but ultimately this proved the most attractive option open to them. The entire Plaxton business, including the sales, service and manufacturing facilities at Anston, were purchased in May 2003 for £10.5 million.

The former Plaxton Wigan plant was less fortunate. Bought by Alexander Dennis, which also took on the Dennis chassis plant in Guildford and the Alexander body-building plant in Falkirk, it continued to produce the President — but only until the start of 2005, when the factory closed and the model was axed. Just over 2,200 Presidents had been built.

The new company — Plaxton Ltd — came into being on 14 May 2004, as a result of the buy-out. Building on the strong foundations laid over the previous few years, it quickly recovered from the effects of six weeks in administration and was soon delivering the complete range — Panthers, Paragons and Profiles from Scarborough, and Cheetahs and Beavers from Anston. Series production of the Pronto minibus started at Anston too. A strong initial order book had been proof of the faith customers had in both the business and its products, and their support during administration and the initial period of

trading was something that was gratefully acknowledged by the new team.

The work done to save the Scarborough factory from closure in 2001 had laid strong foundations which benefited the new business. The production cycle has been reduced from 16 to six weeks. The distance which vehicles travel during the course of production has been cut from five kilometres to one. Stocks of new and used vehicles have been reduced.

The value of the Plaxton name was recognised, and the brand re-established with an updated version of its famous castle logo.

There was a lot of goodwill towards Plaxton and this, coupled to improved product quality and a new 'can do' attitude, saw the revitalised company securing business not only from existing customers but from new customers too.

So, despite having been threatened with closure under the TransBus regime in 2001, Plaxton managed to retain its position as the leading supplier of coaches to operators in Britain and Ireland, and in 2005 supplied just under 300 full-size coaches to operators large and small.

The large operators included First and Stage-coach, and in 2005 both companies took examples of a new generation of wheelchair-accessible coaches from Plaxton. These were

B7R/Profiles which featured a slightly longer front overhang to create the space to include a wheelchair lift in the main entrance. Plaxton had been supplying coaches with centre-mounted lifts for many years, but the accessible Profiles were the first coaches to enter service in Britain (and, indeed, in Europe) that allowed wheelchair passengers to board through the main door. The space on the nearside immediately to the rear of the door was dedicated for wheelchair users.

With interest growing in wheelchair accessibility Plaxton had in 2002 supplied National Express with eight coaches of 12.8m length so that a wheelchair passenger could be carried without reducing the seating capacity. These were Paragons on Volvo B12M chassis and were operated by First between London, Bath and Bristol. The first British coaches to exceed 12m in length, they required dispensation from the Department for Transport.

The length limit was relaxed in 2004 to a new maximum of 15m, and Plaxton was quick to offer the 12.8m Paragon and Panther as part of its standard range. The extra length allowed one more row of seats to be fitted, although in practice many operators stayed with their existing capacity and used the added length to provide more legroom. Because Plaxton's bodies were lighter than those of its competitors it could build 12.8m

coaches on two-axle chassis, confident that when laden they would be able to operate legally within the UK's limit of 18 tonnes gross vehicle weight.

With the business now comfortably re-established the company's new owners started planning new products, announcing two in 2005. The first of these was the Centro, a single-deck bus catering for variants from 10.2m up to 12m — and perhaps beyond if demand warrants it. Announced in May 2005, the Centro programme was to see the first vehicles completed by the end of the year.

Centro was a conventional body, the structure of which was developed from the stillborn Bus 2000 project of pre-TransBus days. The design work was undertaken using the same computer-aided design tools as used for the Panther and Paragon coach ranges. And because vehicles built using this structure had been sold in North America, the basic design had been tested in the USA and was proven in service there.

After launching the Centro on the VDL (formerly DAF) SB120 Plaxton extended its availability to larger chassis including the VDL SB200, Volvo B7RLE and MAN 14.220.

If Centro had taken the industry by surprise, the company's next move was to take it by storm. In early September 2005, the press was assembled in Scarborough for a media briefing at which it

Below: Plaxton was the first manufacturer in Europe to build coaches with wheelchair access by way of the main passenger entrance. To achieve this a wider entrance was necessary with a two-piece door, as seen on this Profile-bodied Volvo B7R for First. Stagecoach also opted for this layout and runs a substantial fleet of accessible Profiles. *Plaxton*

was anticipated that progress on Centro would be the main topic for discussion. But up its sleeve Plaxton had a trump card.

Instead of being updated on the Centro the press were briefed on another bus model — Primo, a new generation of minibus intended as replacement for the huge numbers of Beavers and similar step-entrance products which were now being made obsolete by the demand for low-floor. Not revealed was how far advanced the plan was; Primo was more than paper drawings, and at the conclusion of an address by Brian Davidson and Mike Keaney, the press were suitably surprised by the emergence from a paint bay of a completed vehicle. Volume production was already under-way, and the project had been largely completed with nobody outside the business having any idea of what was being undertaken.

The Primo had been developed in conjunction with Enterprise Bus, a Lancashire company formed by prominent members of the Leyland-based development team of TransBus, which worked with the development team previously associated with TransBus (and Plaxton before it) in Hungary.

Mechanically the Primo had a rear-mounted Cummins engine and a short rear overhang, made possible by the use of a compact RABA driveline. This meant that 19 of the Primo's 28 seats had step-free access. The welded-steel structure was assembled in Hungary and then shipped as a rolling frame to Scarborough, where it was glazed, panelled and trimmed. Bonded glazing was standard, but gasket glazing was offered as an option. The Primo was launched at Coach & Bus 2005 and was widely acknowledged to be one of the stars of the show. The first vehicle, a demonstrator, was used on an accelerated test programme at the punishing Millbrook proving ground, while the second entered service with TM Travel of Chesterfield just a few weeks after the unveiling.

The success of the Primo was followed at the start of 2006 by the unveiling of the first Centro. The first version was a 10.7m midibus on the proven VDL SB120 underframe — and TM Travel was, again, the first customer. The Centro built on Plaxton's considerable experience in the production of aluminium-framed bus bodies — several thousand Pointers over a 12-year period — and also drew on experience in developing Bus 2000.

To handle its diversification into buses Plaxton commissioned a new bus-production plant alongside its existing coach-production facility. This opened in 2006 and operates separately from the coach business. The main shared production facility was the paint spray booths.

Above: A 12.8m version of the Paragon and Panther was added to the Plaxton range in 2004. Park's of Hamilton, one of the first operators of the Paragon when it was launched in 1999, added 10 12.8m Panthers to its fleet in 2006. They were equipped with wheelchair lifts. *Plaxton*

Right: The all-new Primo was unveiled in 2005 with this gold-liveried prototype. The Primo has a rear-mounted Cummins engine and an Allison gearbox, and is manufactured in co-operation with Enterprise Bus of Hungary, which builds the integral frame for completion at Scarborough in Plaxton's dedicated bus-production facility. *Plaxton*

Below: An early user of the Primo was The King's Ferry of Gillingham, which took two in the early part of 2006 for operation on a contracted service between Chatham railway station and a new outlet shopping centre. *Plaxton*

Right: Further broadening the appeal of the Beaver to social services and welfare fleets an updated model was announced in 2005, deliveries starting in 2006. This was the Beaver 3, which combined the established Beaver bus body with the front end of the Cheetah. The London Borough of Redbridge took 11 Beaver 3s in 2007. *Plaxton*

136

Above: The Centro body is offered on a variety of chassis, initial production in 2006 being on the VDL SB120. The first Centro went to TM Travel of Chesterfield. *Plaxton*

Left: The first Scottish buyer of the Centro was Glasgow Citybus, which added three to its fleet in the summer of 2006. They were 40-seaters on VDL SB120 chassis. Glasgow Citybus is a subsidiary of West Coast Motors of Campbeltown. *Stewart J. Brown*

There were further coaching developments in 2006, starting with the option of a wider entrance on the Panther which allowed for the fitting of a wheelchair lift later in the vehicle's life. This increased the length to 12.2m. Operators could, of course, specify a wheelchair lift as part of the original specification if they so chose.

Then came an extension to the company's coach range — quite literally — when it won an order from Stagecoach for 15m-long versions of the Panther. These were for the Megabus express-coach operation and marked the first major order for 15m coaches in the UK, calling for 45. Seating 63, with a toilet compartment at the rear, they were based on the three-axle Volvo B12BT chassis.

To accommodated the longer vehicles a new paint booth had to be installed at the factory. Although Plaxton had built even longer coaches for Stagecoach — 18m-long articulated Premieres in 1995 — these had been painted in two halves so that they could be easily handled in the existing paint facilities.

Today the business employs almost 500 people, and in its first year of trading turned over £47 million — a figure targeted to rise to around £60 million in Plaxton's centenary year.

Construction in progress

Far left: The stainless-steel frame of a Panther on a Volvo B12B

Above: Fabricating a roof structure

Left: Inspecting a completed Panther frame

Above: Profile on a platform in the paint bay

Right: Completed Profile in the paint bay

Plaxton Model Names

Photographs: *Stephen Barber collection, Stewart J. Brown, David Cole, Harry Hay, Roy Marshall, Plaxton.*

Beaver (1986-)
1997 Mercedes-Benz Vario, Stagecoach Manchester.

Bustler (1980-6)
1980 Leyland Leopard, Hedingham & District.

Centro (2006-)
2006 VDL SB120, Arriva North West.

Cheetah (1997-)
2000 Mercedes-Benz Vario, Airlinks, London.

Consort (1955-60)

1957 Bedford SB, Hardwick's Tours, Eston, Middlesbrough.

Crusader (1950/1)

1951 Leyland Royal Tiger, Newton, Conon Bridge.

Derwent (1962; 1966-76; 1986-91)

1972 AEC Reliance, Irvine, Salsburgh.

Embassy (1960-72)

1961 Thames 570E, Mosley, Barugh Green.

Envoy (1950/1)

1950 Maudslay Marathon III, Soames of Ipswich.

Excalibur (1991-9)

2000 Volvo B12T, Nottingham City Coaches.

Highway (1957-66)
1965 AEC Reliance, Bond Bros of Willington, Co Durham.

Panorama (1958-68)
1968 Leyland Leopard, Harris's Coaches, Grays, Essex.

Panorama Elite (1968-75)
1974 AEC Reliance, London Country.

Panther (1999-)
2006 Volvo B12M, Eddie Brown, York.

Paragon (1999-)
2005 Dennis R-series, Alfa Travel, Chorley.

Paramount (1982-92)
1988 Leyland Tiger, Yorkshire Rider.

Pointer (1991-2006)
1998 Dennis Dart SLF, Plymouth Citybus.

Premiere (1991-9)
1995 Dennis Javelin, Vince Coaches, Burghclere.

President (1997-2005)
1999 Dennis Trident, First Centrewest, London.

Prestige (1991-4)
1991 Volvo B12 demonstrator.

Prestige (1991-4; 1997-9)
1999 DAF SB220 (LPG), Arriva Scotland West.

Prima (1997-2003)
2000 Volvo B7R, Marbill, Beith.

Primo (2005-)
2006 Primo, Munro's, Jedburgh.

Profile (2003-)
2005 Volvo B7R, Marshalls, Sutton-on-Trent.

Pronto (2004-)
2005 Mercedes-Benz Sprinter, TransLinc.

Supreme (1974-82)
1977 AEC Reliance, Yelloway, Rochdale.

Venturer (1950-5)
1956 AEC Reliance, Barton Transport, Nottingham.

Verde (1991-7)
1992 Scania N113, Cardiff Bus.

Viewmaster (1977-82)
1982 Leyland Tiger, Fishwick, Leyland.

321 (1990)
1990 Leyland Tiger, Bebb, Llantwit Fardre.

425 (1993)
1993 demonstrator.